The Penland Book
of Glass

The Penland Book *of* Glass

Master Classes in Flamework Techniques

LARK CRAFTS

An Imprint of Sterling Publishing Co., Inc.
New York

WWW.LARKCRAFTS.COM

The Library of Congress has cataloged the hardcover edition as follows:

The Penland book of glass : master classes in flamework techniques / senior editor, Ray Hemachandra.
    p. cm.
  Includes index.
  ISBN 978-1-60059-186-0 (hc-plc with jacket : alk. paper)
  1. Glass craft. 2. Glass blowing and working. 3. Glassware--Study and teaching--North Carolina--Penland. I. Hemachandra, Ray. II. Penland School of Crafts.
  TT298.P45 2009
  748.2028'2--dc22

2008012949

10 9 8 7 6 5 4 3 2 1

Published by Lark Crafts, An Imprint of
Sterling Publishing Co., Inc.
387 Park Avenue South, New York, NY 10016

First Paperback Edition 2011
Text © 2009, Lark Crafts, An Imprint of Sterling Publishing Co., Inc.
Photography © 2009, Lark Crafts, An Imprint of Sterling Publishing Co., Inc.;
unless otherwise specified

Distributed in Canada by Sterling Publishing,
c/o Canadian Manda Group, 165 Dufferin Street
Toronto, Ontario, Canada M6K 3H6

Distributed in the United Kingdom by GMC Distribution Services,
Castle Place, 166 High Street, Lewes, East Sussex, England BN7 1XU

Distributed in Australia by Capricorn Link (Australia) Pty Ltd.,
P.O. Box 704, Windsor, NSW 2756 Australia

If you have questions or comments about this book, please contact:
Lark Crafts
67 Broadway
Asheville, NC 28801
828-253-0467

Manufactured in China

ISBN 13: 978-1-60059-186-0 (hardcover)
ISBN 13: 978-1-60059-679-7 (paperback)

For information about custom editions, special sales, and premium and corporate purchases, please contact the Sterling Special Sales Department at 800-805-5489 or specialsales@sterlingpub.com.

For information about desk and examination copies available to college and university professors, requests must be submitted to academic@larkbooks.com. Our complete policy can be found at www.larkcrafts.com.

Senior Editor: Ray Hemachandra
Editor: Linda Kopp
Art Director: Kristi Pfeffer
Editorial Assistance: Beth Sweet, Amanda Carestio
Art Production Assistance: Avery Johnson
Cover Designer: Kristi Pfeffer

FRONT COVER: Paul Joseph Stankard, *Tea Rose Bouquet Botanical*, 2004, photo by Douglas Schaible

BACK COVER, COUNTERCLOCKWISE FROM TOP LEFT: Emilio Santini, *Goblet* in process, 2008, photo by Steve Mann; Ingalena Klenell, *3 Cylinders I*, 2004, photo by Ragnar Klenell; Elizabeth Ryland Mears, *SHIFT: Bundle for Reaching Skyward*, 2006, photo by Pete Duvall; Shane Fero, *Floral Goblet Grouping*, 2004, photo by John Littleton; Vittorio Costantini, *Monarch Butterfly Life Cycle*, 2001, photo by Eva Heyd

SPINE: Kristina Logan, *Disk Bead Mounted onto Ring*, 2008, photo by Paul Avis

PAGE 1: Shane Fero, *Floral Goblet Grouping*, 2004, photo by John Littleton

PAGE 2: Elizabeth Ryland Mears, *SHIFT: Bundle for Reaching Skyward*, 2006, photo by Pete Duvall

OPPOSITE PAGE: Emilio Santini, *Goblet*, 2000, photo by David Ramsey

Contents

Introduction

Welcome to *The Penland Book of Glass: Master Classes in Flamework Techniques*, the fifth volume in a series produced by Lark Books in collaboration with Penland School of Crafts. These books bring together some of the most important resources of our two organizations: Lark's many years of producing practical books for makers of all kinds and Penland's national community of teaching artists. Penland has long been recognized for the quality and diversity of our glass program, which presents workshops on almost every imaginable aspect of the medium. For this volume we chose to focus on flameworking—the techniques based on heating glass rods and tubes with a torch. This approach to working with glass requires far less equipment, infrastructure, and fuel than hot-glass techniques, while still offering limitless possibilities for expression.

This book has several functions: to give readers insight into the creative processes of leading flameworkers; to provide detailed, intermediate-level technical information; and to showcase a range of approaches to the material. To that end, each of the contributing artists was asked to write an essay addressing her or his personal history, education, sources of inspiration and motivation, or technical approach. These essays are liberally illustrated with examples of each artist's work. They are followed by a "Hands On" section that provides step-by-step instructions for a particular technique or a finished piece. In addition, we have included two beautiful gallery sections showcasing pieces by artists whose flamework has been meaningful to our chapter authors. We hope this book will serve as a valuable technical and inspirational resource for anyone interested in contemporary flameworked glass.

Glass art, traditionally the province of factories and guilds, did not emerge as a craft that could be practiced in small studios until 1962, when Harvey Littleton and Dominick Labino demonstrated using a small-scale glass furnace at the Toledo Museum of Art in Toledo, Ohio. In 1965, Penland's director, Bill Brown, arranged for Bill Boysen, one of Littleton's students, to set up a glass studio at Penland. A week after he arrived, Penland students were making glass. This early embrace of the craft led Penland to become the site of the founding of the Glass Art Society in the early 1970s, and the school has remained strongly identified with the development of contemporary glass. In the years since the first makeshift studio brought glass into the Penland program, we have offered a huge range of classes, including glassblowing, glass casting, glass painting, neon, assemblage, hot

sculpting, mixed media, murrine, canework, Italian techniques, Swedish techniques, many approaches to glass sculpture, and, of course, flameworking.

Flameworking was added to the Penland program in 1986, when Paul Stankard, who wrote the first chapter of this book, was invited to teach a workshop. Within a few years, it was a regular part of the glass program with its own dedicated studio. During the past two decades, our flameworking classes have gained strength and interest as innovative artists—many of them featured in this book—have found ways to increase the scale and complexity of flameworked glass. We've also been able to offer classes that combine the resources of our hot-glass and flameworking studios to create work that would not be possible in either studio alone.

The topics for the book were selected to present a broad range of technical and aesthetic possibilities. Paul Stankard shows some of the methods that go into his famous floral paperweights. Sally Prasch demonstrates the glass lathe, a tool of scientific glassblowers that has not been fully explored by artists. Chapters by Shane Fero and Vittorio Costantini focus on animal forms, both fanciful and realistic. Exploring classic techniques are Kristina Logan, who makes an intricate glass bead, and Emilio Santini, who shows the steps to a perfect flameworked goblet.

Other chapters move away from tradition. Elizabeth Ryland Mears covers surface treatments, including image transfer. Janis Miltenberger creates a large sculpture from multiple parts. Susan Plum demonstrates her glass weaving techniques. And Ingalena Klenell shows how she uses the kiln to expand the possibilities of her torch work.

One of the great strengths of a workshop-based program is that it gives students access to both full-time studio artists who do not teach classes on a regular basis and university faculty who are generally available only to students enrolled in their own programs. Penland teaches classes in books and paper, clay, drawing and painting, glass, iron, metals, printmaking and letterpress, photography, textiles, and wood, and all of our students benefit from having these media taught side by side. Inspiration at Penland also comes from having students of different ages, backgrounds, and levels of experience working together to explore an interest they hold in common. The special learning environment at Penland has, over many years, created a community among the people who teach and learn at the school. It is our hope that these books will bring some of the knowledge and passion contained in that community to a wider circle.

We are grateful to the featured authors for their knowledge, their thoughtful writing, and their beautiful work. They have already contributed to the field through making and teaching, and this book will extend those contributions. We also thank the many other glass artists who allowed us to use photographs of their work. Thanks to Dana Moore, Penland's point person on this project, and to Ray Hemachandra, Kristi Pfeffer, and everyone at Lark Books who put it all together. Special thanks go to Rob Pulleyn, Lark's founder and past president, for bringing this series of books to life.

I feel sure that this book will bring new ideas and inspiration to your work with glass.

Jean W. McLaughlin
Director, Penland School of Crafts

Paul Joseph Stankard

Inspired by nature and the divine, Paul Joseph Stankard creates stunning paperweights with floral themes that often incorporate both sharply realistic and symbolic components. Paul lives the artistic journey, evidenced by risk-taking, originality, and perseverance. He advocates passionately for the fundamental importance of a dedication to excellence in flameworking, art in general, and life.

Tea Rose Bouquet Botanical, 2004
5½ x 2½ x 2½ inches (14 x 6.4 x 6.4 cm)
Flameworked, cold-worked; soda-lime glass
PHOTO BY DOUGLAS SCHAIBLE

Worlds of Glass

My participation in the growth of the flameworking community and teaching at Penland School of Crafts over the years have nourished lasting professional relationships and sweet memories. This essay will highlight many facets of my paperweight-making techniques and artistic philosophy.

For more than 75 years, Penland School of Crafts has been celebrating and promoting beautiful handmade objects. Situated in the Blue Ridge mountain range of western North Carolina, the school is run by kindhearted people dedicated to the educational value of being creative with craft materials.

The school's time-honored philosophy attracts hundreds of students yearly from around the country and abroad. These students are eager to study under gifted studio artists who are considered masters of their crafts. The teachers are influential trendsetters whose artwork evidences impressive standards of excellence and originality within the world of art and craft. The classes are often filled to capacity, and I am especially proud of the glass center's success in offering a diverse range of glassmaking options.

Flameworking first appeared on the Penland campus in the spring of 1977, when Richard Ritter, now a nationally respected studio-glass artist and teacher, invited Hans Godo Frabel to demonstrate his craft to students in the glassblowing concentration. Nine years later, in 1986, Mark Peiser invited me to come to the school and set up a flameworking facility adjacent to the glassblowing area. Penland's first official flameworking session resulted, which in turn ushered in a new wave of creative glassmaking activity.

Most of the more than 30 artists who attended that first session were interested in exploring techniques outside the usual glassblowing methods.

They were eager to learn about flameworking in combination with furnace-working techniques. One of my personal goals was to advocate for the idea that flameworking, which was often thought of as a street craft, is in fact an important glassmaking process. I believed glass paperweights with representational floral themes—the vision I was dedicated to—could rise above kitsch and become a serious part of the studio-glass movement.

My initial Penland experience caused an epiphany: I discovered a new and stimulating creative world outside my studio. This special mountaintop retreat became the art school I never attended, and by teaching and interacting with other artists, my artistic maturity heightened. In my autobiography, *No Green Berries or Leaves: The Creative Journey of an Artist in Glass*, a chapter dedicated to Penland School mentions that first flameworking workshop more than 20 years ago.

Honeycomb Orb, 2004
5½ inches (14 cm) in diameter
Flameworked, cold-worked; soda-lime glass
PHOTO BY DOUGLAS SCHAIBLE

Paul Joseph Stankard

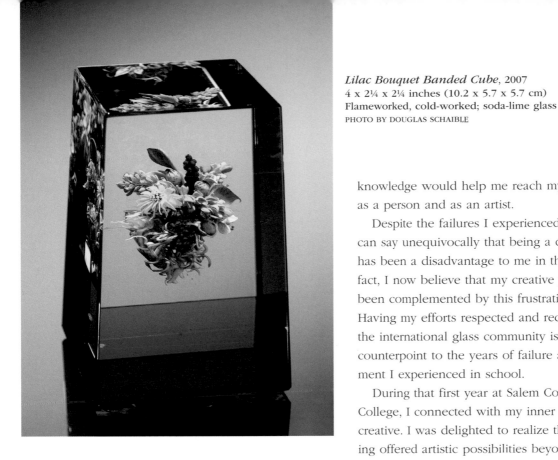

Lilac Bouquet Banded Cube, 2007
4 x 2¼ x 2¼ inches (10.2 x 5.7 x 5.7 cm)
Flameworked, cold-worked; soda-lime glass
PHOTO BY DOUGLAS SCHAIBLE

SCIENTIFIC FLAMEWORK: A CAREER BEGINS

My glass journey began in 1961, when I enrolled at Salem Vocational Technical Institute, which is now named Salem Community College. Its scientific-glassblowing technology program, recently expanded to include glass art, is an exceptional glass program in a community-college setting.

As an eighteen-year-old, I was drawn to this esoteric technical craft after watching students melt glass in glowing flames. It was exciting to realize that deftness and skills were needed to control the danger associated with the process. Salem's glass program was difficult, and I failed scientific glassblowing, as well as algebra, during my first year. These failures were important to me. I found within myself the discipline and ability to persevere.

The reason I was a poor student was because of my undiagnosed dyslexia, a learning disability I found out about years later and one I have spent every day of my life, unknowingly and then knowingly, circumventing.

I love learning. By going to museums, studying art history, and reading literary classics with the aid of audiotapes, I've educated myself as an adult. My education drives my artwork. Since the beginning of my career, I've always believed that seeking

knowledge would help me reach my full potential as a person and as an artist.

Despite the failures I experienced in school, I can say unequivocally that being a dyslexic never has been a disadvantage to me in the studio. In fact, I now believe that my creative journey has been complemented by this frustrating disability. Having my efforts respected and recognized within the international glass community is a touching counterpoint to the years of failure and embarrassment I experienced in school.

During that first year at Salem Community College, I connected with my inner need to be creative. I was delighted to realize that flameworking offered artistic possibilities beyond crafting scientific glass instruments. As a result, I spent the next 10 years mastering my craft, and all the while, I was searching for ways to apply my skills full time on the creative side.

I was introduced to the highly respected paperweight tradition while living and working in and around the South Jersey glass industry. Stories about secretive paperweight glassmakers and how paperweight making required high skill levels, especially when making a Millville rose design, fascinated me.

But because the only paperweight makers whom I knew about in 1969 were, in fact, secretive, I had no one to teach me. I began to work part time in the evenings and on weekends to discover and develop techniques for creating floral paperweights. Through old-fashioned trial and error—and with a big dose of perseverance—I was determined to master this art form. Now, about 40 years later, I am still inspired by the encapsulation possibilities of paperweights, and I hope to continue inventing illusions until I pass on.

Before turning to paperweights, I was working part time, making small glass figurines to earn extra income, but I became bored with giftware and moved into paperweights. I can still remember how excited I would get in the beginning over the smallest success, such as keeping the glass flowers

Paul Joseph Stankard

from distorting or avoiding big air bubbles in the glass. The idea that I was making special things and inventing new techniques kept me interested, and the work became wonderfully satisfying.

This level of interest and satisfaction was a new experience for me. There was something magical about making a colored glass flower suspended in clear glass. Another important aspect of my development at that time was my beginning to share my paperweights with other people and, in the process, learning how much I enjoyed interacting with people while discussing the process and beauty of my artwork.

From 1969 to early 1972, while I was working full time in industry, I was experimenting part time with making paperweights. I would come home from work, have dinner, and then go into the utility room to work. Looking back, what I did meant emotional and financial hardships for my wife, Patricia, as well as for me. I was spending money we didn't have on materials and tools. If it hadn't been for Pat's willingness to make due with less, my artistic career wouldn't have happened.

When I crossed over to the artistic side full time, I realized how beautiful a life working in glass would be, enhanced by the emotional highs experienced with each new discovery. But I now realize that I benefited from my scientific glassblowing experience. I felt comfortable melting glass at the torch, and I understood the glass technology needed to discover and master personal techniques.

By February of 1972, I felt secure enough with paperweights to quit my full-time job. On my first day on my own, I thanked God for the opportunity to begin my dream work. I never looked back.

MY PHILOSOPHICAL FRAMEWORK

I believe the surest path to personal success in art making is to develop techniques that celebrate one's special world. When teaching, I tell students to risk taking a big leap over the traditional vocational approaches in hopes of inventing new skills for making their own art.

To inspire my paperweights, I draw on memories of growing up in rural Massachusetts. As a child, I loved living close to what seemed like an endless forest outside my back door. I spent hours of playtime discovering and being fascinated by

nature's infinite mysteries. Now, as an artist, my references to the mystical memories of the quiet woods bring magical realism to my glass. My challenge is to disguise the difficulty of the process that makes the work happen.

Ultimately, in my work, I'm trying to celebrate the mysteries of sex, death, and God. I start my day with a prayer and think of my labor as a continuation of that prayer, as if it were a repeated mantra. My flameworking bench has symbols on it, including a Catholic crucifix, miniature statues of deities, and Greek Orthodox icons, to remind me that God respects one's best efforts. This belief is important to me because it unites the spiritual with my intellect and emotions while I am melting glass in the flame. I idealize artists as being like nuns or monks in their studios—making beautiful objects as prayers.

The three primary ingredients that I strive for in my work are beauty, which evidences spirituality; skilled virtuosity, which evidences truth to the material; and making art personal, which evidences originality.

Today my inspiration comes from listening to the words of classic books and from the work of poets such as Walt Whitman, just as much as it does from walking in the woods. My emotional and philosophical needs are reflected in language layered over nature, which I've practiced in recent work. I believe glass is the perfect material for celebrating and interpreting nature's primal beauty.

I encourage my students to survey art history and to blend it into their contemporary efforts. Doing so keeps the work connected to the past, while giving the made object a fresh point of view. Another approach is to be curious and to seek new techniques. To make glasswork personal, you must be willing to invest days and even years of emotional energy in your work.

As an artist, I've spent most of my time solving technical problems while pushing to create new three-dimensional illusions suspended in clear glass. I've taken creative and technical risks, and I've learned from my countless failures. For me, this work is all about persevering while I search to develop a new visual language.

The artistic journey is difficult and unpredictable, and it requires both courage and strength to believe in your vision.

Paul Joseph Stankard

Floating Bouquet Orb, 2006
8 inches (20.3 cm) in diameter
Flameworked, kiln cast, constructed; soda-lime glass
PHOTO BY DOUGLAS SCHAIBLE

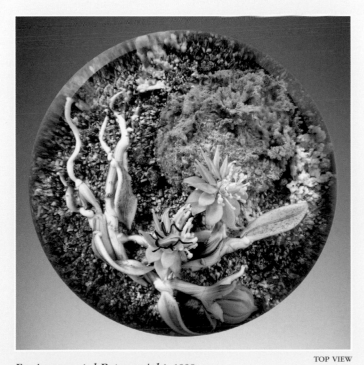

TOP VIEW

BOTTOM VIEW

Environmental Paperweight, 1998
3¼ inches (8.3 cm) in diameter
Flameworked, cold-worked; soda-lime glass
PHOTOS BY DOUGLAS SCHAIBLE

Paul Joseph Stankard

Swarming Honeybee Orb, 2006
5½ inches (14 cm) in diameter
Flameworked, cold-worked; soda-lime glass
PHOTO BY DOUGLAS SCHAIBLE

THE STATE OF THE FIELD

Today's growing interest in flameworking is responsible for exciting new works that are having an increasing impact on the glass-art landscape. The idea of flameworking as an artistic process must sometimes seem odd to newly initiated practitioners, especially those who have first encountered its street-craft incarnation. However, I believe flameworking offers creative people the opportunity to discover innovative ways in which to express ideas in hot glass—and to do so economically.

Flameworking is going through a colossal change in the hands of high-energy young artists who are challenged by this centuries-old craft. Today, many people are beginning their creative journeys with BFA and MFA degrees that encourage a fine-arts expectation to hover over the work. As a result, we're seeing fresh efforts, including some that are conceptually challenging. These new works are attracting international attention from serious collectors and museum curators.

An artist friend once jokingly referred to glassblowing as a team sport. When I heard her analogy, I immediately began to think of flameworkers as solitary long-distance runners. I've been involved with flameworking for more than 45 years and can remember when very few runners were on the track. I'm amazed at the evolution—and revolution—this process is experiencing in the hands of artists who push the technique's boundaries and potentials. I often think about how exciting it will be in the years to come, as we all experience the significant works that will evolve out of these new explorations in creative glass activity.

Flameworking is attracting literally thousands of creative people—mostly in the United States—who want to master a craft in order to work hot glass. Because of its appeal, a new industry is growing. Magazines, newsletters, and Internet chat rooms are dedicated to the technique. Manufacturers are responding to the needs of flameworkers by developing specialized tools and equipment. I predict that this approach to glassmaking will eventually displace glassblowing as the preeminent creative center of hot-glass activity.

In Eugene, Oregon, possibly the flameworking capital of the world, a great concentration of glass artisans is engaged in melting glass at the bench. These hundreds of glassmakers bring high energy and talent to the production of decorative pipes, bongs, and a wide variety of street-craft items. It's just a matter of time before some of these creative counterculture glassmakers, challenged by the process's possibilities, go beyond drug and sex paraphernalia to impact the creative glass landscape. The best of the Eugene flameworkers are already attracting the attention of collectors, who are purchasing their borosilicate glass art objects.

EXCELLENCE FIRST

While teaching a class at Penland recently, I wrote on the blackboard: *Don't blame the process for stupid work.* I recounted for my students a conversation I once had with studio artist Ginny Ruffner, who takes advantage of the flameworking process. She and I were at the Pilchuck Glass School in Stanwood, Washington, in the late 1980s. I was teaching, and Ginny was an artist in residence. Ginny said, "Lampworking is thought to be the bastard stepchild of glassblowing." I heard her statement and burst out laughing, because I had felt those negative sentiments in the glass-art world for a long time.

Paul Joseph Stankard

Now, years later, what I printed on the blackboard has become common wisdom, thanks to a lot of talented people in art centers such as Penland School of Crafts. We no longer dismiss a process such as flameworking because of the insignificant glass it might generate; instead, we look at the artistic maturity of the work.

When I have the good fortune to visit The Corning Museum of Glass in Corning, New York, I'm both humbled and inspired by the great work in the museum's remarkable collection. I marvel at significant examples of flameworked objects created without the modern technological advantages offered by computerized annealing ovens, gas-oxygen torches, and compatible clear and colored glasses. I'm perplexed, intrigued, and challenged when I think about how most contemporary flameworked objects pale in comparison with the flameworked glass that has survived from centuries past. I include much of my own work in this statement. We can all do better.

I recently attended a wholesale show and stopped to admire flameworked goblets that were beautiful and well crafted, only to be told by the artisan that they didn't sell well. He said, "This year I'm hoping to be successful with my long-stem glass flowers in glass vases." The fellow went on to say, "I love making goblets, but the orders are slow coming in. I want to figure out what will be salable in the craft galleries."

On my way home, I thought about my new, young acquaintance and my own early years of working to advance my craft without the comfort of making money. By setting out to be successful in the marketplace, you enter a design category with different criteria to follow. You can be known as an artist making one-of-a-kind objects or as someone who produces multiples. This choice is important and personal, and it will dictate your journey.

But I believe being successful is about excellence and committing your talent to developing and refining work that is meaningful, regardless of the marketplace. Excellence transcends categories, and great work attracts attention.

DEDICATION

In 1986, I met a holy man at Penland whose inner beauty touched my soul. This chapter is dedicated to Penland elder statesman Paulus Berensohn, a clay artist and teacher who has touched the lives of thousands of people worldwide.

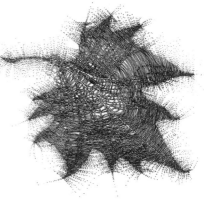

PAULUS BERENSOHN
Sycamore, Late Fall, 2000
6½ x 7½ inches (16.5 x 19 cm)
Doodle; pen and ink

Paulus celebrates the virtues of working by hand to make art that leads to emotional growth. During his four decades at Penland, Paulus has invited sympathetic people to feel the poetry associated with the earthen material in the service of craft and to internalize the hand-heart process of making things. His personal philosophy speaks to the healing virtues of beauty and to the creation of objects as a sacred act.

Paulus' life has been dedicated to a mystical journey while working in clay, and his vision has heightened Penland's sense of purpose. He has challenged my own creative impulse to be stronger and more courageous. Thank you, Paulus, for sharing your gift and beautifying our artistic landscape.

Cornflower Bouquet with Honeybee and Figures Orb, 2005
5½ inches (14 cm) in diameter
Flameworked, cold-worked; soda-lime glass
PHOTO BY DOUGLAS SCHAIBLE

Hands On

Paul Joseph Stankard has interpreted
nature through glass for more than
four decades. He demonstrates how
to create and encapsulate a floral
paperweight design.

1 This oven, which I use for reheating and
annealing, is essential to my process. I reheat
sections of large, colored glass rods and clear glass
gobs to 1000°F (538°C) and redraw the rods down
to smaller rods for flameworking. Here, to preheat
the clear glass gob that I'll later ball up at the torch
and use to encapsulate my paperweight design, I
place it in the oven.

2 Material preparation, which dominates my
craft, is illustrated here as I melt colored glass and
roll it in glass powders for variations in color.

Paul Joseph Stankard

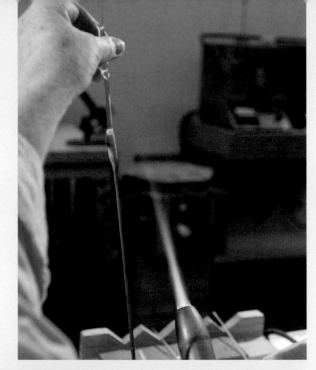

5   After the flower's stamens are sealed around the pistil ...

3   The results of this coloring are mottled materials that will be used to make leaves, stems, petals, and berries.

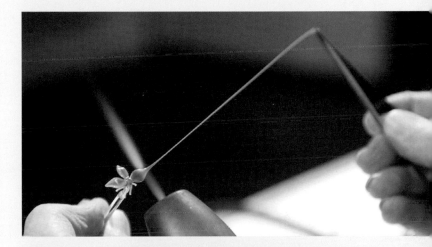

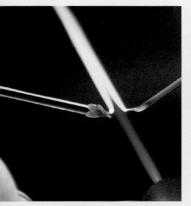

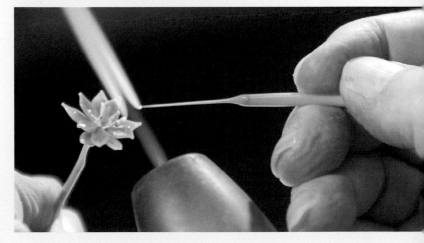

6   ... the petals are sealed in place. A stem is then fused to the back of the flower, and when the anthers are melted on, the flower is complete.

4   To suggest negative space, the colored glass is melted over a clear glass rod, illustrated here as I build a flower bud. By melting the clear glass rod to separate it from the colored glass and adding a green stem, a bud is formed.

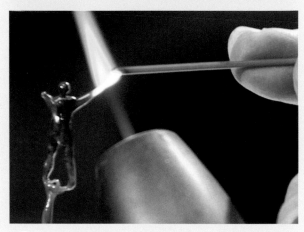

7 I'm sculpting a small-scale human form, which will be incorporated into the root system of the flower.

9 The colored glass components are fused together with a needlepoint flame, in the design laid out in the previous step.

8 When laid out, the colored glass components suggest how the flowering plant will be interpreted when the pieces are encapsulated in clear glass.

10 I begin to build the contents of the pickup plate by filling it with crushed glass. This glass will provide the background color for the flower.

Paul Joseph Stankard

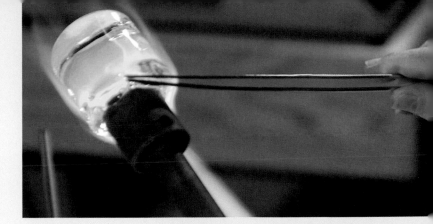

11 The flower is placed on the glass in the pickup plate …

12 … and the pickup plate is surrounded by the pickup cup. Everything is ready for encapsulation.

13 Clear glass, beaded on the end of a pontil, …

14 … sticks to a clear glass gob removed hot from the oven.

15 The gob is melted into a ball of glass so that it can be dropped on top of the colored glass design in the next step.

16 The ball of glass is dropped into the pickup cup.

17 The colored glass and flower are now encapsulated by the clear glass, and the whole piece is lifted out of the pickup cup.

18 The piece is melted smooth.

21 The form is shaped in a rectangular mold.

22 A second pontil is added to the bottom to hold the piece ...

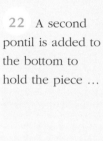

19 While I was working on the top half of the paperweight, I had an assistant making the bottom. My assistant now hands me the clear-glass bottom half.

23 ... so the top can be shaped and finished once the first pontil is removed.

20 The two halves are melted together, and the colored glass is fully sealed in clear glass.

THE PENLAND BOOK OF GLASS
Paul Joseph Stankard

24 The piece is knocked off the pontil and into the oven to be annealed.

25 After the piece is annealed, it is ground and polished to produce the finished paperweight.

26 Here's a view of my workbench and tools after the paperweight has been made. All of my tools are very modest.

About the Artist

A pioneer in the studio-glass movement, Paul Joseph Stankard has established an international reputation for interpreting nature in glass with his floral art. His career has spanned more than four decades. Paul remains active in the studio, while teaching at institutions such as Penland School of Crafts, Pilchuck Glass School, and Salem Community College. He has been tireless in promoting flameworking throughout his career.

Paul has written an autobiography, *No Green Berries or Leaves: The Creative Journey of an Artist in Glass*. Born in North Attleboro, Massachusetts, in 1943, he now lives in Mantua, New Jersey, with his wife, Patricia. They have five children and six grandchildren. In addition to continuing his own work, Paul is mentoring the efforts of his children and glass artist David Graeber, as the next generation at Stankard Studio.

Paul's work is represented in more than 40 museums worldwide, including the Renwick Gallery of the National Museum of American Art in Washington, D.C.; the Victoria and Albert Museum in London; the Musée des Arts Décoratif in Paris; the Hokkaido Museum of Modern Art in Sapporo, Japan; the Tittot Glass Art Museum in Taipei, Taiwan; the Metropolitan Museum of Art in New York City; The Corning Museum of Glass in Corning, New York; and the Museum of American Glass in Millville, New Jersey.

He has received an Artist as Hero Award from the National Liberty Museum in Philadelphia; a Lifetime of Innovative Achievements in Art Award from the Art Alliance for Contemporary Glass in Chicago; and an UrbanGlass Award for Innovation in a Glassworking Technique from UrbanGlass in Brooklyn, New York. He has received honorary doctorates from Muskingum College and Rowan University. Paul was elected to the College of Fellows of the American Craft Council in 2000.

Golden Orb Column, 2002
7 inches (17.8 cm)
Flameworked, cold-worked; optical glass
PHOTO BY JOHN HEALEY

Shane Fero

Birds, fantastic archetypal figures, and shadow boxes are among the series Shane Fero has pursued in his dynamic explorations of color and form. Informed by a thorough study of the history of the glass arts, Shane brings a sense of playfulness and joy to his thoughtful, beautiful flameworked designs. His meditative survey of birds offers a window into how a single topic can invite endless variation and innovation during an artistic career.

The Conversation about Eggs, 2005
5 x 8 x 3½ inches (12.7 x 20.3 x 8.9 cm)
Flameworked, acid etched; soft glass
PHOTO BY TOM MILLS

In 1968, I was a 15-year-old living in Winter Haven, Florida, near the Cypress Gardens adventure park. I would often ride my bike over to The Amazing Howell's Glassblowing Shop to watch Bob Howell demonstrate his skills.

When Bob and his wife, Marie, retired, Jerry and Lee Coker bought the shop. I befriended Keith, Jerry's son, who introduced me to his father and stepmother. The next thing I knew, I was mowing their lawn and doing odd jobs for them. And within two or three months, they started teaching me flameworking techniques.

I worked for them after school and on weekends, moving along what I now consider to be a traditional apprenticeship path. When Jerry and Lee sold the store to one of their students, Roger Smith, the choral director at Winter Haven High School, I carried on under him throughout the rest of my high-school and community-college years. I even lived with the Smiths while I was going to college, and I demonstrated flamework techniques at Cypress Gardens, where I eventually helped them set up a glass shop.

Jerry and Lee moved around a bit. They settled in Keeseville, New York, near Lake Champlain, and set up a flameworking concession at Ausable Chasm, a stone canyon that was established as a tourist attraction way back in 1870. They were planning to set up another concession at Santa's Workshop in North Pole, New York, and they invited me to come up and participate in this venture during the summer of 1974.

I took a sabbatical from Cypress Gardens and moved to the Adirondacks to demonstrate flameworking as one of Santa's elves. I loved living in the mountains, so I decided not to return to Florida.

I enrolled in the philosophy program at Plattsburgh State University, and I worked glass in Peru, New York, at Jerry and Lee's winter studio.

During the next couple of years, I worked at Santa's Workshop and Ausable Chasm during the summer, and the Peru workshop in the winter. During this period, I also spent a lot of time hiking and camping in the mountains and observing birds. I joined the Audubon Society and began a life list for the identification of birds. These years and experiences were the birthplace of my fascination with birds.

After I had lived in the Adirondacks for about a year, I was talking to friends one night about how I wanted to render philosophical, mythological, and psychological ideas with my flameworking techniques. Because I really enjoyed the process of working glass on a torch, I thought I should integrate all the elements of my life and express all my interests in my glass efforts. This framework for

Lauschan Yellow and Green Fat Finch, 2006
4 x 7 x 3¼ inches (10.1 x 17.8 x 8.3 cm)
Flameworked, acid etched; lead and soda-lime glasses
PHOTO BY TOM MILLS

my glasswork has stuck with me. Expressing myself with my medium—actually making objects that reflect my interests—is a fantastic way to earn an income and foster a lifestyle and career.

Working on a torch—being mesmerized by the flame and by the transformation of rods and tubes into objects of my own design—is fun and challenging, as well as meditative. As my skill levels have increased, and my ideas morphed and coalesced, I have experienced a fantastic journey. My work never bores me because there is always room for improvement and a constant flood of new ideas. The transformation of a hard material—softening and melting it, and manipulating it by sculpting or blowing—reminds me of alchemy.

Not only did this process fascinate me, as it does now, but demonstrating it in front of people who were equally enthralled only bolstered my resolve to continue along this line of work. I still feed off the symbiosis of the performance of the maker and the energy, interest, and enthusiasm of the audience. I teach and demonstrate at various symposia, conferences, and institutions throughout the world. When I began this journey, I never imagined it would evolve into the work I do today, with its reach around the globe, but dedication and persistence brought my work to fruition and acceptance.

Pseudo Thrushes with Eggs & Jumbo Blueberries, 2005
Tallest bird: 5 x 8 x 3¼ inches (12.7 x 20.3 x 8.3 cm)
Flameworked, acid etched; lead and soda-lime glasses
PHOTO BY TOM MILLS

A PROCESS OF DISCOVERY

People often ask me when I began making birds, and I have to say, "Almost immediately." In my glassmaking career, I have always created birds of some sort, whether solid or blown. A big impetus to make birds came in 1977 when I opened my gallery, Classical Glass, in Plattsburgh, New York, with my partner and apprentice, Tim Tiernan. Freed from my own apprenticeship relationship, I made about 60 bird species in likeness, using solid rods of glass in the 1- to 2-inch (2.5 to 5.1 cm) range. I usually mounted these birds on wood branches, in a diorama format.

My newfound freedom allowed me to make whatever interested me. Besides blown vessels and abstract sculptures, I went wild trying to execute all sorts of animals and creatures. I proceeded through the entire animal kingdom—hoofed animals, African animals, dog breeds, mammals, the human form, fish, and other marine life—and then even through the plant kingdom, making trees, mushrooms, and other plant life. You name it, and I have probably tried to make it.

Sculptural experimentation was good training for me in form, motion, and space, as well as color, surface decoration, and texture. I relied on photographs, field guides, and observations in nature itself for my models. I think it is very important to study a subject in depth, and to research how other people in the history of art and craft have expressed similar subjects.

Floral Goblet Grouping, 2004
Tallest: 12 x 3¼ x 3¼ inches (30.5 x 8.3 x 8.3 cm)
Flameworked, acid etched; lead and soda-lime glasses
PHOTO BY JOHN LITTLETON

Untitled, 2006
11 x 3¼ x 3¼ inches (27.9 x 8.3 x 8.3 cm)
Flameworked, acid etched; lead and soda-lime glasses
PHOTO BY TOM MILLS

Bamboo Series Goblets, 2004
Tallest: 11 x 3¼ inches (27.9 x 8.3 cm)
Flameworked; lead and soda-lime glasses, fused gesso
PHOTO BY JOHN LITTLETON

Later, during the late 1980s, I started making human-hybrid mythological sculptures that reflected my interest in surrealism and mythology. These efforts energized me and enabled me to express a lot of creativity. I have been an aspiring Egyptologist since I was about nine years old. The ancient Egyptian pantheon of gods and goddesses who combine human and animal forms has always fascinated me. At sixteen, I also became enamored of the work of Salvador Dali, who was inspired by his dreams and hallucinations. Working with glass rods to create both human and animal forms—as inspired by my own imagination—started me on my path. Also, because I always loved to dance, I put dance gestures and movements into my hybrid figurative sculptures, giving them a sense of fun and natural power.

All that said, one major event provided the catalyst for making these forms. After my partner, Tim Tiernan, and I went our separate ways in 1980, I wasn't really sure what he was making because he wouldn't send me any images of his new work. I was occasionally sending him slides of my work, and I think this lack of reciprocity started to bother me subconsciously. One night I dreamt I visited his house. I went down to his basement studio and was awed by all the sculptural figures he had made in various colors. I was at once proud of and intimidated by them and him.

After I woke up, I really thought about those sculptures, and I subsequently started making them myself. A couple of years later, I visited Tim and his family. Of course he didn't make anything like what I had dreamt about, but my feelings of insecurity, as processed through my subconscious, had provided me with a wealth of ideas. It was almost as if I had started to compete against the fruits of my own imagination.

In fact, ever since then I have continued to dream about going into someone's gallery or studio—or my own—and seeing pieces that excite and inspire me. The pieces that I see are probably a combination of things I have seen perceptually, but they are reconfigured in my subconscious. In one dream, I was looking through a coffee-table book of paintings that impressed me. When I looked at the cover to find out who the artist was, I was surprised to find out it was me.

I even dreamt that I made large Barbie dolls! My daughter, Devon, had a collection of them. I didn't then actually make Barbie dolls—just as I haven't made some other objects I have seen in my dreams—but they all continue to be a fountain of creativity for me in my surrealistic method.

MY PENLAND EXPERIENCE

I took my first class at Penland School of Crafts in 1988, as a student of and assistant to Fred Birkhill, and then I took my first glassblowing class under Stephen Dee Edwards. Although I had been working in flameworking techniques since 1969, joining the Penland School community was the most consequential event in my whole career.

The next year, I returned to Penland as a visiting artist for Fred, and then I took a class under Paul Marioni later in the summer. By the summer of

Klee Bird, 1999
19 x 10 x 8 inches (48.3 x 25.4 x 20.3 cm)
Flameworked, sandblasted; borosilicate glass
PHOTO BY JOHN LITTLETON

Shane Fero

Madame Magritte, 1998
16 x 8½ x 8½ inches (40.6 x 21.6 x 21.6 cm)
Flameworked, sandblasted; borosilicate,
lead, and soda-lime glasses
PHOTO BY JOHN LITTLETON

*The Modern Woman
Executive,* 1991
12 x 8 x 5 inches
(30.5 x 20.3 x 12.7 cm)
Flameworked, sandblasted;
borosilicate glass
PHOTO BY JOHN LITTLETON

1990, I was co-teaching with Fred. Following that class, my wife, Sallie, and I moved to Penland, North Carolina, for good. At that point in the school's history, there was only one class in flameworking each summer—our class alternated with one taught by Paul Stankard. Being the only flameworker living near Penland allowed me to help develop the full, vital flameworking program the school has today.

Before I started at Penland, I had a good career, mostly doing craft fairs and gallery exhibitions, but encouragement and advice from Fred and Paul Marioni put me on a more audacious path. For one thing, Fred taught me how to expedite many techniques I was aware of or had tried at one time or another, but had struggled with in execution.

Fred continues to share a wealth of information in his teaching, and he has been highly influential in the flameworking world. By using a painterly approach to the application of powder and shards, Fred applies many techniques borrowed and adapted from the hot-glass world and also from the art world in general. He emphasizes the idea of utilizing flameworking together with mixed-media techniques. Doing so gives the work a larger context and perspective, for artists and viewers alike.

In that first class back in 1988, Fred gave students an assignment to make a shadow box. This assignment referenced Joseph Cornell, the mid-twentieth century artist who assembled wood, glass, and other found objects to contextualize themes and subject matter. I did not actually produce a shadow box until 1993. But since then, the boxes have formed an ongoing body of work for me. In 2004, my birds became the theme of such boxes, and I am still exploring this series enthusiastically.

Shane Fero

FOR THE BIRDS

The birds for which I became well known were actually an outgrowth of a technique I was taught early in my apprenticeship. I would blow the shapes of birds from tubes and utilize rods of glass to add appendages or details, such as wings, feet, eyes, and beaks. Historically, this technique was primarily used in Bohemia, Germany, and Austria. It made its way over to the United States in the late nineteenth century and twentieth century.

When I was younger, I used this technique to make doves, owls, geese, swans, and penguins. Today I would consider the birds I made then, as well as most of the ones I saw produced by other artists, to be very kitschy. However, since then I have seen fine work done with that technique, in Lauscha, Germany, and also by Jaroslav Brychta.

In 2000, I taught at UrbanGlass in Brooklyn, New York, and I was provided with a short residency during which I worked with a gaffer, Rob Panepinto. We produced a few large bottles on which I flameworked surface designs. I finished off the bottles by making stoppers that were human-animal hybrids. When I returned to North Carolina, I started a series of bottles with John Geci, a young, talented glassblower who lives in the Penland community. I cold-worked the bottles, sandblasted them, and finally acid etched the surfaces. I then made flameworked stoppers; each was attached to a branch with a bird on it. Later, I started adding a flower to the branch as well. The birds on these branch stoppers each had only one leg, which was fused to an appendage on the branch.

Speculum Alchemaie, 1993
13½ x 21 x 11 inches (34.3 x 53.3 x 27.9 cm)
Flameworked, sandblasted; borosilicate and plate glasses
PHOTO BY JOHN LITTLETON

Shane Fero

The Exploration of the Mysteries of Plant and Animal Life, 1996
17 x 17 x 3¾ inches
(43.2 x 43.2 x 9.5 cm)
Flameworked; soda-lime and plate glasses, wood, paint, manipulated images
PHOTO BY JOHN LITTLETON

Because of the economic slump in the art market after the terrorist attack of September 11, 2001, I searched for something to make that was a little lower in price range. In 2002, John Cram, the owner of the Blue Spiral 1 gallery in Asheville, North Carolina, invited me to participate in a group exhibition with the theme of birds. I came up with the idea of making my birds actual bird size—larger than they had been on the bottles—and letting them stand on their own two feet. I used all the gesture, surface decoration, and formal space that I had learned from years of experience and gathering new techniques, but I was trying to make something that could be recontextualized with a contemporary twist. For me, the birds symbolized freedom and spirituality, which gave me—and I

hope others—an uplifting sense of being that countered the malaise of the post-9/11 blues.

The greatest thing about the subject of birds is that a series based on them is unlimited in creative scope—open to endless explorations and variations. I can reference actual species of birds; create birds out of my imagination; place them in settings or groupings with fruits, eggs, or other objects; or place them in shadow boxes. The possibilities are always challenging because of color variations, improvements in my skill level, and new glass products that can affect the outcomes. I am never bored with the birds or with the process of research, design, and execution.

Because I travel a lot, I have been privileged to see birds in different parts of the world. It is

Shane Fero

Play, Play, Play..., 2003
17 x 17 x 3¾ inches (43.2 x 43.2 x 9.5 cm)
Flameworked; soda-lime and plate glasses, wood, acrylic paint
PHOTO BY JOHN LITTLETON

Some Kind of Thrush, 2008
3½ x 7 x 3 inches (8.3 x 17.8 x 7.6 cm)
Flameworked, acid etched; lead and soda-lime glasses
PHOTO BY TOM MILLS

always a joy to see a member of a species that's new to me, in its natural setting, displaying a furtive move of its head or a flick of the tail. Such a discovery inspires me and freshens my perspective about birds.

I have a library of bird books, including field guides and coffee-table books, from all over the world, as well as bird prints by Louis Agassiz Fuertes and John Audubon, bird photography by Eliot Porter, and books that include poems and writings about birds. One of my favorite books is *A Convergence of Birds: Original Fiction and Poetry Inspired by the Work of Joseph Cornell*, edited by Jonathan Safran Foer. Each chapter is written by a different author and preceded with a print of one of Cornell's bird boxes. Also, I never tire of perusing the book *Joseph Cornell*, edited by Kynaston McShine and published by The Museum of Modern Art.

The study of art history, philosophy, mythology, and literature—and, for me, ornithology—are essential to round out an artist's perspective for creating work. One of my favorite artists is the late Morris Graves, the Pacific Northwest painter who is especially well known for his depictions of birds and flowers. The mystical, spiritual, and sublime aspects of his birds transcend mere representation. It is this spirit that I aspire to in my own work. Such Graves paintings as *Blind Bird, Bird Singing in the Moonlight,* and *Spirit Bird* capture an essence and vulnerability that are hard to define and very moving. Other artists who have had a lasting influence on me are Paul Klee, Salvador Dali, Pablo Picasso, William Blake, and Hieronymus Bosch. Of course, I may be influenced just as much by literature, music, or anything I find in my natural or unnatural surroundings.

In the late 1980s, while I was at a craft fair in Florida, someone told me my work reminded him of the work of Miro, the great Spanish painter and sculptor. Inexplicably, Miro was someone I hadn't taken much notice of before. So I researched him and quickly found out what the person meant.

Ever since, Miro's childlike approach to art and his wonderful sense of color and form have had a profound effect on me, and it shows in my work. The primacy of his forms has influenced my sculptural sense. Whenever I need inspiration, I pull out one of the many books I now have about Miro. I am always recharged.

My wife and I used to take care of an Amazon double yellow nape named Pete. Pete could say about 500 words and put together syntax in eerily intelligent sentences. Because we enjoyed that bird-sitting, we decided to adopt cockatiels and, later, a few parakeets. Today, we have one cockatiel, Ubie, a male; we have had him for more than 20 years.

Living with a bird is very stimulating for my work and gives me immediate observation of bird movement and gesture. Ubie's behavior always shows real character and humor, whether he is dancing to rock or blues, improvisationally whistling to Miles Davis, or tracking an intruding insect with a quizzical, beady eye.

LOOKING TOWARD THE FUTURE

I have been very fortunate to have a long career in flameworking, glassblowing, and other mediums related to my work. Working with other materials and techniques—including wood, stone, vitreographs, painting, drawing, and collage—has enriched my whole experience. Exploring other mediums and experimenting with them is beneficial because they can play off one another. Painting canvases influences the surface decoration of my birds and vessels, for example, and the reverse is also true.

Adding new bodies of work is sometimes very challenging, but it keeps me on the cutting edge of the field. All new work is in essence a problem-solving activity. To reinvent oneself and one's work is the most rewarding aspect of an artist's life. Some new bodies of work require assistance or collaboration, and I also find these joint efforts rewarding, not just for the finished work but also for the stimulation of the collaboration.

Besides continuing to work on the birds and revisiting my existing bodies of work, I will be making a new series in collaboration with glass artist Eddie Bernard. During the summer of 2006, along with a team at The Studio of The Corning Museum of Glass in Corning, New York, we started making larger-scale blown and flameworked glass branches in the hot shop. We continued the process at Penland School of Crafts and now meet and work whenever we can. The created branch is then cold-worked and usually cut on a saw, sandblasted, and acid etched; then Eddie adds a metal armature so the branch can be mounted on a wall. Later, I add birds or other parts, mounting them on the branch in drilled holes.

I also wish to continue a collaboration started at Pilchuck Glass School, where I taught in 2003, making my figurative gods and goddesses in a much larger format with a team in the hot shop. We have only made two so far, but I've been very excited by the results.

In closing, I want to emphasize one more time how important it is for flameworking students and artists to study the history of art and the glass arts. Too many flameworkers are somewhat ignorant of those histories. Sometimes, remarkably, people believe they have invented or discovered new techniques and ideas that have been around for thousands of years.

Part of the problem is that flameworking is not included in most university glass programs. Mostly, flameworking is taught in the workshop format. However, flameworking students coming out of university art programs should have at least some art history in their backgrounds. I advise any student of the glass arts to study their history and the history of art in general. Glass-art traditions should be acknowledged and honored—and their rules should sometimes be broken in order to realize a meaningful creative progress.

Bird Spirit Vessel, 2008
7½ x 2½ x 2½ inches
(19.1 x 6.4 x 6.4 cm)
Flameworked, acid etched;
lead and soda-lime glasses
PHOTO BY TOM MILLS

Shane Fero

Hands On

Shane Fero is best known for his avian creations. He demonstrates how to make a bird from simple glass tubing, using the flame and his breath.

1   I pull a point on a 1-inch (2.5 cm) tube of lead-based glass by first heating a section approximately 1¼ inches (3.2 cm) long uniformly in the flame and then pulling outward evenly while rotating the tube so that the pulled part is on center and long enough—8 to 9 inches (20.3 to 22.9 cm)—to serve as a punty (or handle) for the piece. Heating and pulling another section of the tube, away from the area already pulled, yields another punty at the other end of a center section. The center section I'm making is 3½ to 4 inches (8.9 to 10.2 cm) long.

2 I heat the completed center section, rotating it in the flame uniformly from shoulder to shoulder so the heat is distributed evenly.

3 Rotating the glass very smoothly, I lightly roll the heated center section in a glass powder that has been mounded in the center of a plate. Applying too much pressure can disfigure the glass walls, so I use a light touch.

4 I roll the center section in a second powder …

5 … and a third powder, striving to achieve a nice gradation of color.

6 Melting and applying a stringer of glass, pre-pulled from a larger rod, is one way I draw designs.

7 I also add design with shards of glass, which I apply with tweezers. In most cases, the shard is not preheated; as its edge is heated, it adheres to the glass. I make the shards in advance by blowing glass on a blowpipe and then breaking the blown glass into pieces.

8 After the shards have been heated and fused in place, it's important to regain a roughly uniform wall thickness in the piece; when you add layers of color, the glass becomes irregular in depth. Heating it to regain uniform thickness will ensure that when the piece is later blown out, it does so predictably.

9 Melting glass rods is another way to draw designs. Here, I'm using German hot-glass bars, which I've pulled into rods.

10 I fuse the designs all the way into the piece. Again, I take care to even out the wall thickness.

11 To separate the tail section from the main body, I melt the glass down, constricting it by rotation, gravity, and the flame, and then separate it with a pull. The head section is separated from the main body in the same fashion.

12 I heat up the main body in preparation for …

13 … blowing out the body of the bird. Unlike making a vessel form, during which process you apply pressure or use hand manipulation to keep the piece uniform, you're actually doing an asymmetrical blow here in order to achieve the shape of the bird. It's not only my breath that shapes the body; gravity and the way I'm moving my hands as I'm blowing are also important.

Shane Fero

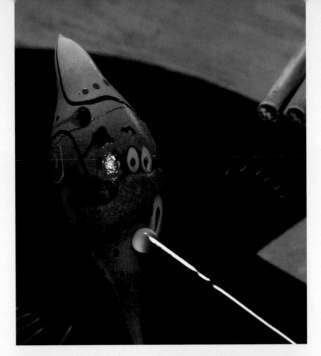

14 I use a mini squasher to flatten the tail.

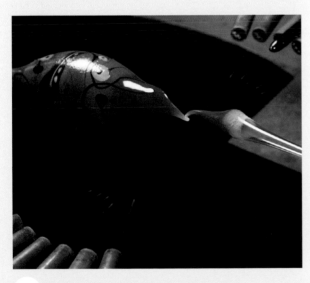

15 The head is formed by tapering down one point and twisting the punty off.

16 To make the first leg, I take a solid black rod, heat the end of it so it's molten, and then apply it to the blown form, which has been spot heated. I blow through a hollow—the punty—to form the leg at the point of the molten glass. (The upper portion of the leg becomes hollow, usually down to about the joint; the lower portion remains solid.) Blowing out the second leg in the same way—to "solid seal" it—is the most difficult step of the whole process for me. When applying this leg, I have to be careful not to spot-heat the first leg area inadvertently, or the first leg might strain or crack.

Shane Fero

17 I flame anneal the body and legs with straight propane. You can also use natural gas. Carbon forms on the piece because you've gone below the strain point of the glass. If carbon isn't forming, you're above the strain point of the glass.

20 The bird's head is flame annealed.

18 I add the eyes with a glass rod …

21 To remove the punty from the tail, I spot-heat the section I want to break off and use thin tweezers that have been immersed in room-temperature water.

19 … and also use a rod to create the beak.

22 I add the feet by melting a rod …

Shane Fero

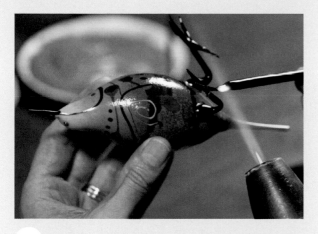

23 ... and then add the toes in the same fashion.

24 The finished bird will be annealed in a kiln. I bring the temperature up at a moderate pace from room temperature to 825°F (441°C) and hold it there for 15 minutes. Then I turn off the kiln. I almost always finish the bird by acid etching it with an acid-etching cream.

About the Artist

Born in Chicago, Illinois, in 1953, Shane Fero has been flameworking since 1968. He frequently lectures and conducts demonstrations at international symposia and conferences. Shane has taught at a wide array of institutions, including Penland School of Crafts in Penland, North Carolina; UrbanGlass in New York City; Pratt Fine Arts Center in Seattle, Washington; The Studio of The Corning Museum of Glass in Corning, New York; the University of Michigan; Eugene Glass School in Eugene, Oregon; Espace Verre in Montreal; Pittsburgh Glass Center in Pittsburgh, Pennsylvania; Pilchuck Glass School in Stanwood, Washington; Bild-Werk Frauenau in Frauenau, Germany; and the Niijima Glass Art Center in Niijima, Japan. He has also taught at the International Festival of Glass in Stourbridge, United Kingdom; and the Glass Art Society Conference in Seto, Japan.

Shane's work is found in the collections of private and public institutions worldwide. Since 1992, he has held more than 20 solo exhibitions, and he has participated in more than 400 group exhibitions during his career. Shane has been honored with retrospectives at the Alfred Berkowitz Gallery at the University of Michigan–Dearborn and the Huntsville Museum of Art in Huntsville, Alabama. His work can be found in more than 20 museum collections, including those at the Museum of Arts & Design in New York City; Glasmuseum in Ebeltoft, Denmark; the Asheville Art Museum in Asheville, North Carolina; the Huntsville Museum of Art in Huntsville, Alabama; Museum für Glaskunst Lauscha in Lauscha, Germany; the New Orleans Museum of Art in New Orleans, Louisiana; and the Niijima Glass Art Museum in Niijima, Japan.

Shane is president of the board of directors of the Glass Art Society. He maintains a studio in Penland, North Carolina, next to Penland School of Crafts.

Blue Jay Babe, 2005
17 x 10 x 6 inches
(43.2 x 25.4 x 15.2 cm)
Flameworked; borosilicate glass
PHOTO BY TOM MILLS

Kristina Logan

If beads, which have been made for art and adornment throughout human history, each say something about the era in which they were created, Kristina Logan's exquisite flameworked beads should make us optimistic about how our times will be remembered. Kristina's beads are classically gorgeous—bold, colorful, and precise. Curiosity about technique has led her to marry glass and metal in her inspired jewelry designs.

Candlesticks, 2004
13 x 4½ x 4½ inches (33 x 11.4 x 11.4 cm)
Flameworked, cast; soda-lime glass, bronze
PHOTO BY PAUL AVIS

How did I become an artist? I have a very clear memory of a bright yellow necklace in my mother's jewelry box. The beads were opaque glass, and they were made to look like some kind of fruit—perhaps lemons. I remember wondering how they were made, and yet I was convinced that I knew how the forms were dripped into place. I remember tapping them on my teeth and knowing that this was the sound that glass made. It was still a mystery to me how the beads could look so liquid and be so rigid at the same time.

My mother was a graphic illustrator, and she raised my brother and me on her own. She sometimes had full-time jobs; at other times, she moved from one freelance job to the next. When she worked at home, I remember standing nose-level to her drawing table and watching her closely. I was always sure to hear "Don't bump the table!"

Seeing my mother work made me realize at a very young age what I wanted to do when I grew up: I wanted to make things with my hands. Somehow, I knew it was possible—in fact, I had no doubt I could do it. She did it, after all. My mom gave me this confidence.

I studied fine arts at the University of New Hampshire. I fell in love with figure drawing, sculpture, and the problem solving involved in creating three-dimensional objects. After school, I worked in a café baking bread and serving coffee. I also kept a little studio, in which I carved big wood figures with a chainsaw.

My glass education came completely by accident. Someone walked into the café one day and offered me a job working for a glass artist. The offer came like this: "Don't you know who Dan Dailey is?" I didn't. I didn't really care that he was a glass artist and, as it happened, one of the leading contemporary glass artists in America. I was simply interested in earning a living by working for an artist, no matter what he or she made.

I worked for Dan Dailey for four years. I experimented with pâte de verre for my own wood sculptures, but during most of that time I never felt that glass would become my primary medium. Working with hot glass seemed too complicated for me to want to try. The process involved way too many tools and people. The great gift of working in Dan's studio was that I was able to participate in so many levels of the glassmaking process: from cold-working to analyzing why something cracked; from installing architectural commissions to packing pieces so they would arrive undamaged at far-off destinations. I did just about everything, right down to spending many days and weeks enameling with a sharpened toothpick.

Ivory Brooch, 2001
2¾ x 2¾ x ½ inches (7 x 7 x 1.3 cm)
Flameworked; soda-lime glass, sterling silver
PHOTO BY PAUL AVIS

MY SPIRITUAL CONVERSION

After three years of working with glass for Dan, late one evening during a glass-casting workshop, I saw someone flameworking. I remember watching one bead being made before I was shooed away. I was thrilled and amazed: You could work hot glass by yourself? No large studio? No assistants running around?

After seeing just this one demonstration, I soon started flameworking in my own studio. I bought a small torch and gathered from friends all the other equipment I needed: glass, hose, regulators, and safety glasses. Beads were the first objects I made, and only because I didn't know how to make anything else. For about a year, I carried those first little misshapen beads in my pockets wherever I went.

I was fascinated by my first, imperfect attempts at melting glass on my own. The beads I made led me to an interest in *all* beads. I became obsessed with them and learned as much as I could about their history, where different beads came from, what they were used for, and why they were important to so many cultures around the world. I was delighted to learn that beads were used as religious objects to keep track of prayers and mantras; as monetary exchange (they were sometimes traded for gold, raw gems, and even human slaves); and purely for decoration by both the very wealthy and the very poor.

I started seeing my own beads as sculptural objects for the human body. I saw myself being part of the world through my beads, connecting to people past and present.

I call this period of time, when I began making beads with more conviction, my "spiritual conversion." At first I meant this in a tongue-in-cheek way, but the conversion was serious. I started studying ancient and antique beads and collecting them from all around the world during my travels, as well as from bead trade shows and antique shops. The old beads fascinated me. It's not that I wanted to recreate what I found; I was just inspired by

Sophia Necklace, 2007
⅜ x ⅜ x 17½ inches (1 x 1 x 44.5 cm)
Flameworked; soda-lime glass, sterling silver
PHOTO BY DEAN POWELL

how these tiny objects traveled through time—worn close to the skin and passed from one person to the next, surviving for hundreds and even thousands of years.

In addition to the beads I was constantly looking at—and still find inspiration in today—I started studying architectural details, Renaissance and pre-Renaissance mosaics, and religious reliquaries of the 1300s to 1500s. I am inspired by all patterns that I see. I love objects that are based on repetition and dot patterns, and I translate this approach into my own beads.

When I was accepted into the Contemporary Glass Bead Exhibition in 1993, at the Bead Museum in Prescott, Arizona, I was nicknamed the "Dot Queen" by fellow beadmakers at the show. Mostly, the name was a means of identification—at that time, almost everyone could be described in a

Kristina Logan

Amber Box, 2002
4 x 4 x 4 inches (10.2 x 10.2 x 10.2 cm)
Flameworked, pâte de verre; soda-lime
glass, lead crystal, sterling silver, fine silver
PHOTO BY PAUL AVIS

Amber Tea Pot, 2000
6½ x 6½ x 3¾ inches (16.5 x 16.5 x 9.5 cm)
Flameworked, pâte de verre; soda-lime glass,
lead crystal, sterling silver
PHOTO BY PAUL AVIS

Kristina Logan

Ivory Totem Brooch, 2001
4½ x 1¾ x ½ inches (11.4 x 4.4 x 1.3 cm)
Flameworked; soda-lime glass, sterling silver
PHOTO BY PAUL AVIS

DEEPENING MY WORK

Can injury bring about something positive? My years of obsessive production beadmaking induced arthritis in my left thumb. I realized—or at least, my doctor did—that I could not go on producing beads in the same way without doing more harm to my hand. Basically, I was told that I needed to move my hands in a different way, or I wouldn't be able to continue working.

It never occurred to me to stop beadmaking or to find another profession. In order to manage the pain in my hands, I sought out acupuncture and began practicing yoga regularly. These two practices continue to help me find balance in my life. Still, the pain in my hands forced me to rethink what I could do with my beads, instead of just producing them for other people to use.

word or two, according to the kinds of beads they made—but my label stuck. The Society of Glass Beadmakers, which is now called the International Society of Glass Beadmakers, was created by the group of glass artists gathered at the exhibition. I served as president of the organization from 1996 to 1998.

Soon after the show closed, I traveled around the country in my Volkswagen van for more than six months, making and selling beads. By calling up beadmakers, introducing myself, and visiting their studios, I witnessed the beginning of the contemporary glass movement in action. I slept in beadmakers' driveways from Virginia to California.

I met a great, diverse collection of people, all of whom were passionate about glass beads. Eventually I settled down and spent the next 10 years making beads in my own New England home studio. To this day, I work from home in New Hampshire and sometimes in France, where my husband is from, and I teach internationally.

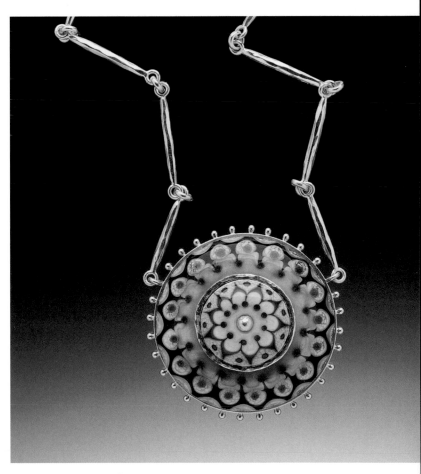

Ivory Pattern Brooch, 2007
2¾ x 2¾ x ½ inches (7 x 7 x 1.3 cm)
Flameworked; soda-lime glass, 18-karat gold
PHOTO BY DEAN POWELL

Kristina Logan

Ivory Textured Brooch, 2000
2¼ x 2¼ x ½ inches (5.7 x 5.7 x 1.3 cm)
Flameworked; soda-lime glass, sterling silver
PHOTO BY PAUL AVIS

Olive Cactus Bead, 1997
1¾ x 1⅝ inches (4.5 x 4.2 cm)
Flameworked; soda-lime glass
PHOTO BY PAUL AVIS

Violet Brooch, 2003
2¾ x 2¾ x ½ inches (7 x 7 x 1.3 cm)
Flameworked; soda-lime glass, sterling silver
PHOTO BY PAUL AVIS

What did I want to make next? This was a hard question for me, and somehow I thank my hand injury for making me stop and think.

My first ideas were based on jewelry. How did I want my beads to relate to the human figure? I have always been fascinated by ornamentation and by how objects relate to the human form, but I had never made jewelry before. I went back to the roots of my interest: Beads are fundamental objects in body adornment. I also wanted to do something unexpected with my beads, so I began to employ unconventional ways of putting the beads together. Instead of just stringing my beads, I was cutting, grinding, or polishing them, or sometimes using a combination of these approaches.

I like to say that I learned metalworking by osmosis and soldering over the telephone. I'm not a trained metalsmith. Initially, I started making jewelry by collaborating with a jeweler friend. One day, when she was not available in person, I forged ahead by designing a piece that she explained to me how to make. Cutting, filing, and sanding metal seemed straightforward enough. I looked at soldering as just another way to use a torch, but to melt metal instead of glass.

Yes, I made many mistakes. But to this day, I work in about the same fashion. I design a piece that I want to make. If I can't figure out how to make it on my own, I call a colleague and ask her or him how I should make it. I am deeply grateful

for these relationships—I could name names, but the list would be tremendously long.

I confess that my method comes with big advantages and disadvantages. Unfortunately, sometimes it takes me twice as long—or more—to accomplish a task that a trained jeweler could complete in minutes. But sometimes I do things in innovative ways that other people might consider impossible, and that is the incredible gift of working like this. No one gets to tell me, "You can't do that," so I feel very free.

I also began making other objects at about this time. I had always wanted to try using beads as ornamentation for objects independent of the human form. I like to start with the simplicity of a bead and to use it, or multiples of it, to embellish an object. I now make objects—candlesticks, containers, boxes influenced by religious reliquaries, and vessels such as teapots—that relate back to the human form.

Technically, I love combining materials, especially metal and glass. When it's hot, glass can be so soft and pliable, and when it's cold, it can be shiny and seductive. Metal is hard, structured, and opaque. The challenge comes when these two materials meet. How do you put them together, physically and aesthetically? My work explores the connection points of these very different materials.

In addition to my flameworking, I cast bronze and work with silver. I constantly face the technical

Kristina Logan

challenge of coping with the fragility of glass where it meets metal. Will the glass crack when I put the materials together? I am always searching for innovative ways to pair glass and metal. I make tiny handmade screws, hide fabricated cotter pins, or gently hammer seemingly impossible bezels around glass objects. A clean, simple connection thrills me.

A TEACHER'S PHILOSOPHY

I began teaching just about as soon as I could make a bead by wrapping glass around a mandrel successfully. I taught what I myself knew at the time. This is still the basis of my teaching today, and, happily, I know more now than I did then!

I teach in hopes of sparking a light within students so that they can create what is inside them to create. I often teach specific techniques in my beadmaking classes, but it isn't my students' execution of these techniques that most interests me. The lessons are really ways for me to describe how I use my hands, how I use the flame, and how I use the glass. Yes, it is true that all of this is technical information, but my hope is that I can give students the technical information and the resources they need to become more independent in their work. That is the practical part of my teaching. In the big picture, I do not care whether students can make perfect replications of what I show in class. I care more deeply that they understand how they can move the glass and their own hands in the ways they want them to move.

My greatest hope is that my students' work will improve with this information. Information becomes knowledge when it is digested completely. The hard work begins when students go home to their own studios, and they are faced with making what is inside their heads and hearts to make. I cannot be a source for their inspiration. I hope only to be available for encouragement—and to offer a spark.

Finding your own voice is the hardest job. No one can tell you what your personal voice is. Discovering it takes listening quietly, a willingness to experiment, and the courage to take paths that have no precedent.

There is no right way or wrong way to go. As I have discovered for myself, what seems to be the wrong way becomes the right way. I wish many good things for my students and for all those who *make*. Follow your own path and, mostly, you will find joy.

Abstract Ivory Pattern Constellation Necklace, 2007
½ x 2 x 24 inches (1.3 x 5.1 x 61 cm)
Flameworked; soda-lime glass, sterling silver
PHOTO BY DEAN POWELL

Kristina Logan

Hands On

Kristina Logan, the "Dot Queen," demonstrates how to make a disk bead and mount it onto a ring.

1 The tools in my flameworking area and on my bench include my GTT Lynx torch. Ninety percent of my beads are made with Effetre soda-lime glass. The rod rack was given to me by Vittorio Costantini. I rarely use it to warm up my rods as I work; the rack ends up being another way to hold the glass I'm working with at any given time.

2 I start by making a round bead. I'm using transparent cobalt glass. The first wrap of glass determines the thickness of the final disk. I take care to keep the glass smooth around the hole in the bead, so there will be no sharp edges around it.

4 I heat the bead quickly and aggressively on one side only, and then shape that hot side with a graphite marver. I want the opposite side to stay rigid, so it will provide some resistance when I use the marver on the hot side. If both sides become hot and start to move, the bead will lose its shape and may break free of the mandrel; then I'd have to start all over again. I take care not to direct the flame into the bead's hole, because I want it to retain its smooth edges.

5 I flatten the other side with the marver, controlling the heat in the same way as in the previous step.

3 I continue to build the base of the disk bead with transparent cobalt glass. I'm careful not to use too much heat, or the bead will become round in shape and not disk-like. These first several wraps of glass establish the diameter of the bead.

6 I do some final shaping by adding glass wherever it is needed to make the outer circle completely round. The bead's shape must be corrected at this stage. Any "out of roundness" in the bead now will be amplified in the final disk and will distort the final design and pattern. If I am making multiple beads of the same shape and size, this is also the stage at which I check the bead's diameter with a caliper, as shown.

Kristina Logan

7 Using an opaque, lapis-colored glass, I add dots to the circumference of the piece. These dots are the most important ones on this bead, in terms of the placement of the design. I concentrate on the negative spaces between the dots just as much as I concentrate on the amount of glass I'm applying to make each dot. I keep the glass rod the same temperature throughout the dotting process.

8 The first row of dots is my guide for placing the interior dots. At this point, I decide whether or not to decorate both sides of the bead. Sometimes I make a complete bead by dotting both sides. At other times, especially when I know I want to use the bead for jewelry, I only decorate one side and leave the opposite side "blank." The blank side is the side that I grind and hide against the finished metal.

9 I add another layer of opaque, light-turquoise dots to achieve the final turquoise color that I want in the finished bead.

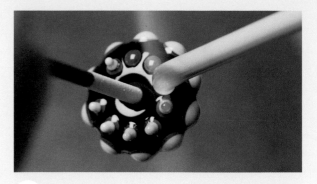

10 I continue adding the second layer of opaque dots on top of all the original dots. I'm decorating both sides of this bead equally.

11 When I want to make very small dots on my beads, I first shape my glass rod to a point on the graphite plate that I keep in front of my torch. I don't use stringers for my dotting. Sharpening the end of a glass rod to a point enables me to create very small dots by heating the tip of the glass.

12 Using the sharpened rod, I place small dots between the existing dots. I heat only the very tip of the rod. I use the first two layers of dots as guides to the placement of these small dots.

13 Using a ³⁄₁₆- to ¼-inch-diameter (5 to 6 mm) rod of glass, sharpened to a point, allows me to get into tight places on a very big, hot bead. Here, I'm adding very small dots around the bead hole.

14 Once I've added all the base dots, I start heating them evenly, melting them all at the same rate before adding the next layer.

15 I add transparent dots on top of the existing opaque dots, giving the transparent glass rod a firm push in order to have it cover as much of each base dot as possible.

16 I add transparent dots to all the opaque dots, including the smallest ones. The amount of glass added and the original spacing of the dots will determine the pattern they'll form when they melt together. The tighter the dots are placed together and the greater the amount of transparent glass used on each one, the tighter the final pattern will be. Surface tension squeezes the dots into other shapes, such as diamonds and squares. Finding the right amount of glass and spacing for the desired effect takes experimentation and practice.

17 During final heating and shaping, it's important to heat the bead evenly so that the pattern comes out evenly. All shaping is done as lightly as possible so the pattern is not smeared or distorted. I use a graphite marver, which glides smoothly over the glass and does not distort the design. Do not rush this final process! I like to say to students, "You have worked very hard to get to this point, so why rush the final five minutes?"

18 I'm careful to check for any defects. Once I consider the bead to be finished, it's ready for the kiln.

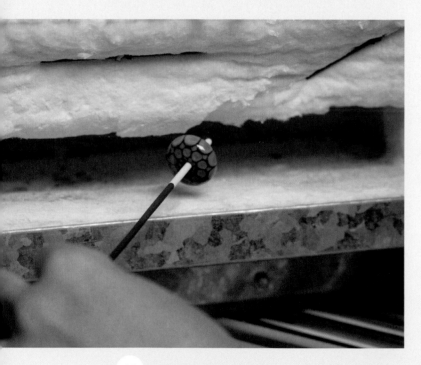

19 I anneal all my beads in a small kiln made specifically for beadmaking.

20 Once the bead is out of the kiln and cold, I select the side that I want to display in the final piece. I carefully grind the opposite side flat, using a flat lap grinder designed for cold-worked glass.

21 This side of the disk bead is ready for placement.

22 I make a ring of silver from 12-gauge round wire; it fits loosely around the bead and functions as a kind of faux bezel. I sometimes keep the ring smooth; at other times, I make hammer marks to create decorative effects. I leave a little space around the bead so that when I grind a little more from its back, it will fit snugly in the ring, without gaps.

Kristina Logan

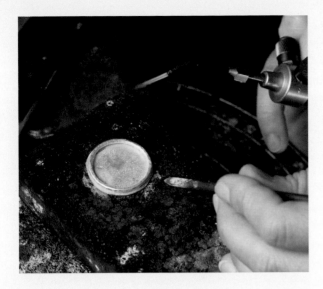

23 The silver ring is soldered onto a flat piece of 24-gauge silver. I use hard solder so that it won't melt when I make more solder joints later on.

24 I use a tap to cut tapered threads inside a silver tube. This takes some experimentation. Here, I've found the right-sized tap for the size of silver tube I want to use. I'm using a 4-40 tap for ⅛-inch (3.2 mm) heavy wall tubing.

25 To create the threads on a silver wire, I'm using a 4-40 die that corresponds with the tap that I just used for the tube. This way, the threaded wire will screw into the silver tube. I'm using 10-gauge wire.

26 I solder the threaded wire onto a finial. Sometimes, I make a simple finial. At other times, I make a more complex pattern and bigger finial by soldering jump rings together and then hammering a pattern on them with chasing tools; the jump rings become part of the finial. In either case, the final result is a little handmade screw.

29 When I polish all the silver parts, I sometimes use a patina of liver of sulfur, which remains in the crevices of the silver and gives the metal some contrast.

27 I solder the threaded tube to the ring using medium solder. It's important to take care not to flood the inside of the threaded tube with too much solder, or you won't be able to twist the screw into the tube smoothly. Because I solder the tube in the center of the ring, the bead must have a hole that is perfectly centered in order to fit onto it. If a bead hole is made off-center, the tube must also be soldered on off-center, so the bead will fit the placement.

30 When I do the final fitting of the bead into the ring, I sometimes have to make small adjustments to the bead by grinding the bottom a little more so that the bead will fit as tightly as possible, without any gaps visible around its edges.

28 The ring shank is soldered onto the back of the ring. The soldering of the ring is now complete.

31 I double-check the ring for its final polish, patina, and bead fit before I apply thread-locking glue to the threads. Once I apply the thread locker, I have only one shot at threading the piece together. The glue begins to harden with the friction created by screwing the two pieces together, so before I apply the thread locker, I practice several times to make sure all the pieces fit perfectly. Sometimes I have to shorten the screw or file the tube a bit in order to fit the finial properly against the bead. When the piece is threaded together, the ring is finished.

About the Artist

Kristina Logan is recognized internationally for her glass beads and, specifically, for the precision of her work. She served as president of the International Society of Glass Beadmakers from 1996 to 1998.

"Beads are part of my lifelong fascination with art and ornamentation," she says. "Glass beads form a historical thread, connecting people and cultures throughout our history. I feel that my beads place me on this timeline—connecting me to the past and present."

Kristina was one of only four artists whose work was selected for exhibition in the Smithsonian American Art Museum's *Renwick Craft Invitational: Four Discoveries in Craft, 2002*. "Logan's beads exist in their own right as art," wrote Kenneth Trapp, curator-in-charge at the Renwick Gallery. Articles about Kristina's work have appeared in numerous publications, including *Glass Magazine, Ornament, Beadwork, Bead & Button, Lapidary Journal,* and *La Revue de la Céramic et du Verre.*

Kristina loves to travel, both professionally and for pleasure. She travels extensively throughout the United States and Europe, teaching workshops and lecturing on contemporary glass beads and jewelry. She hopes to inspire glass beadmakers with her teaching and her work. Kristina has taught beadmaking at such well-known schools as The Studio of The Corning Museum of Glass in Corning, New York; UrbanGlass in Brooklyn, New York; Haystack Mountain School of Crafts in Deer Isle, Maine; Penland School of Crafts in Penland, North Carolina; Musée-Atelier du Verre à Sars-Poteries in Sars-Poteries, France; and Centro Studio Vetro and Abate Zanetti International Glass Center, both in Venice, Italy.

Kristina primarily works in New Hampshire, where she lives with her husband and two children, and she sometimes works in Provence, France, where she and her husband met.

Persian Brooch, 2001
2¾ x 2¾ x ½ inches (7 x 7 x 1.3 cm)
Flameworked; soda-lime glass, sterling silver
PHOTO BY PAUL AVIS

Our 10 chapter authors were asked to commend artists whose flamework uses similar techniques to their own. The artists featured in the two Gallery sections were selected by at least one—and often by several—of the chapter authors. The impressive array of work presented here attests to the diverse creative possibilities the torch offers glass artists.

ALBRECHT GREINER-MAI
Cup and Vase, 1983
Tallest: 10⁷⁄₁₆ inches (26.4 cm) high
Flameworked, montage technique; thread glass
PHOTO BY LUTZ NAUMANN
COLLECTION OF MUSEUM OF GLASKUNST, LAUSCHA, GERMANY

ALBRECHT GREINER-MAI
Cup and Vase, 1994
Tallest: 8½ inches (21.6 cm) high
Flameworked, montage technique; thread glass
PHOTO BY LUTZ NAUMANN
COLLECTION OF MUSEUM OF GLASKUNST, LAUSCHA, GERMANY

ALBRECHT GREINER-MAI
Galaxies, 1996
Tallest: 7⁵⁄₁₆ inches (18.6 cm) high
Flameworked, montage technique; thread glass
PHOTO BY LUTZ NAUMANN
COLLECTION OF MUSEUM OF GLASKUNST, LAUSCHA, GERMANY

JAY MUSLER
Breezy, 2004
9¼ x 6½ x 3½ inches (23.5 x 16.5 x 8.9 cm)
Flameworked, sandblasted, oil painted;
borosilicate glass
PHOTO BY ARTIST

JAY MUSLER
Winter Starburst, 2007
9 x 8 x 3 inches (22.9 x 20.3 x 7.6 cm)
Flameworked, sandblasted, oil painted; borosilicate glass
PHOTO BY ARTIST

JAY MUSLER
Sad But Funny, 2007
9 x 5 x 5 inches (22.9 x 12.7 x 12.7 cm)
Flameworked, sandblasted, oil painted;
borosilicate glass
PHOTO BY ARTIST

JAY MUSLER
Red Rabbit, 2007
11 x 4½ x 3½ inches
(27.9 x 11.4 x 8.9 cm)
Flameworked, sandblasted,
oil painted; borosilicate glass
PHOTO BY ARTIST

JAY MUSLER
Turntable, 2007
4 x 22 inches (10.2 x 55.9 cm)
Bowl: Gravity shaped, sandblasted,
oil painted; soda-lime glass
Hooks: Flameworked, sandblasted,
oil painted; borosilicate glass
PHOTO BY ARTIST

JAY MUSLER
Starfields, 2008
4 x 22 inches (10.2 x 55.9 cm)
Bowl: Gravity shaped, sandblasted, oil painted; soda-lime glass
Hooks: Flameworked, sandblasted, oil painted; borosilicate glass
PHOTO BY ARTIST

ANDRE GUTGESELL
Ice, 2006
6¹¹⁄₁₆ x 10⅝ x 5⅞ inches (17 x 27 x 15 cm)
Flameworked, montage technique; soda-lime glass,
mounted on a glass plate
PHOTO BY ARTIST

ANDRE GUTGESELL
Color Light, 2007
Tallest: 11⁷⁄₁₆ inches (29 cm) high
Flameworked, montage technique, engraved;
soda-lime glass
PHOTO BY LUTZ NAUMANN

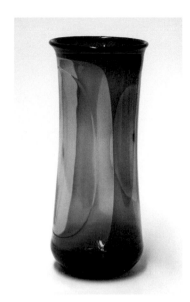

THOMAS MULLER-LITZ
Goblet, 2004
16 inches (41 cm) high
Flameworked, montage technique;
Lauscha color soft glass, solid and
striped glass
PHOTO BY LOTHAR BIRTH

THOMAS MULLER-LITZ
Vessel, 2005
7½ inches (19 cm) high
Flameworked, montage technique;
Lauscha color soft glass
PHOTO BY LOTHAR BIRTH

THOMAS MULLER-LITZ
Vessel, 2005
5¾ inches (14.5 cm) high
Flameworked, montage technique; Lauscha color
soft glass, striped glass
PHOTO BY LOTHAR BIRTH
COLLECTION OF MUSEUM BAD FRANKENHAUSEN, BAD
FRANKENHAUSEN, GERMANY, AND MUSEUM LÜNEBURG,
LÜNEBURG, GERMANY

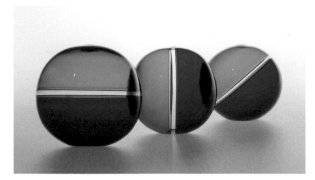

ANDRE GUTGESELL
Intersections, 2006
Largest: 9¹³⁄₁₆ inches (25 cm) in diameter
Flameworked, montage technique; soda-lime glass
PHOTO BY ARTIST

ANDRE GUTGESELL
Differences, 2005
Each: 3¹⁵⁄₁₆ inches (10 cm) in diameter
Flameworked, montage technique; soda-lime glass
PHOTO BY ARTIST

HEATHER TRIMLETT
Blue Bicycle Series, 2007
Largest: 2 x ⅜ inches (5.1 x 1 cm)
Flameworked, detailed, ground, polished; soft glass
PHOTO BY MELINDA HOLDEN

HEATHER TRIMLETT
Primary Vessel Series, 2006
3 x 1¾ x 1⅝ inches (7.6 x 4.4 x 4.1 cm)
Flameworked, hollow formed, detailed;
soft glass, marble
PHOTO BY MELINDA HOLDEN

PRISCILLA TURNER SPADA
Antiqued Bead Cuff Bracelet, 2005
2 x 2½ x 1⅛ inches (5.1 x 6.4 x 2.9 cm)
Flameworked, textured, hand fabricated; soda-lime glass,
enamels, baking soda, sterling silver, sterling silver spacer
beads and wrapped wire
PHOTO BY PIERRE CHIHA

TOM HOLLAND
Untitled, 2005
1 x ¹⁵/₁₆ x ⁷/₁₆ inches (2.6 x 3.4 x 1.2 cm)
Flameworked; murrini cane, soda-lime glass
PHOTO BY ARTIST

TOM HOLLAND
Disc with Stars and Cross, 2003
1¾ x 1¾ x ⁷/₁₆ inches (4.5 x 4.5 x 1.1 cm)
Flameworked; murrini cane, soda-lime glass
PHOTO BY ARTIST

PRISCILLA TURNER SPADA
Blueberry Brooch, 1999
2¾ x 2⅛ x ¾ inches (7 x 6.1 x 1.9 cm)
Flameworked, textured, oxidized; soda-lime glass,
sterling silver, copper leaves, patina
PHOTO BY PIERRE CHIHA

TOM HOLLAND
Untitled, 2002
1¼ x 1¼ x ⅜ inches (3.2 x 3.2 x 1 cm)
Flameworked murrini; foil, soda-lime glass
PHOTO BY ARTIST

MASAMI KODA
Link, 2002
24 x 9 x 9 inches (61 x 22.9 x 22.9 cm)
Flameworked; glass, copper wire, steel
PHOTO BY YUJI UCHIDA

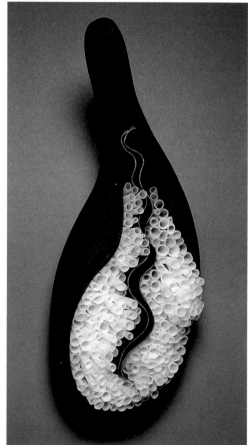

MASAMI KODA
Koto Koto, 1997
6 x 15 x 5 inches (15.2 x 38.1 x 12.7 cm)
Flameworked; glass, wood, feathers
PHOTO BY YUJI UCHIDA

MASAMI KODA
Forming, 2002
15 x 5½ x 7½ inches (38.1 x 14 x 19 cm)
Flameworked; glass, wood, copper sheet, silicon carbide
PHOTO BY YUJI UCHIDA

MASAMI KODA
Orbit, 1998
17 x 12 x 6 inches (43.2 x 30.5 x 15.2 cm)
Flameworked; glass, copper, pulp
PHOTO BY YUJI UCHIDA

MASAMI KODA
Red Dew 4, 2007
14 x 14½ x 10 inches (35.6 x 36.8 x 25.4 cm)
Flameworked; bronze, cast glass, silver, borosilicate glass
PHOTO BY YUJI UCHIDA

MASAMI KODA
Drip in the Dark, 2005
20 x 14½ x 8½ inches (50.8 x 36.8 x 21.6 cm)
Flameworked; steel, silver, copper wire, glass
PHOTOS BY RUSSELL JOHNSON

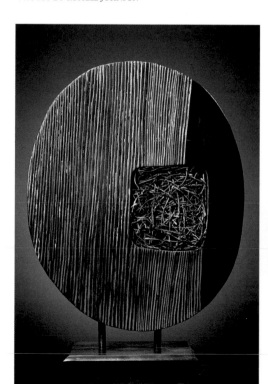

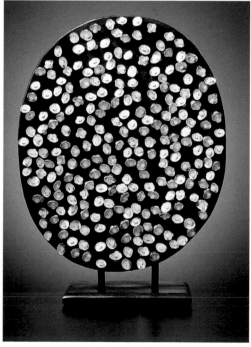

DINAH HULET
Lynn: Image/Self-Image, 1998
12 x 27 x 1½ inches (30.5 x 68.6 x 3.8 cm)
Flameworked, murrine; soda-lime glass
PHOTOS BY P. HULET

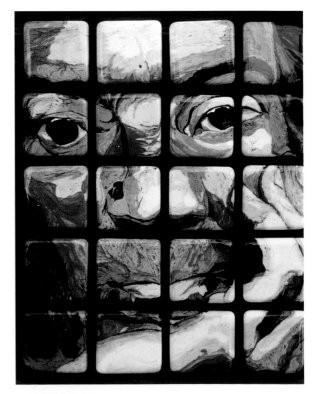

DINAH HULET
PS '96 (component study), 1998
Largest: 1³⁄₁₆ inches (3 cm) diameter
Flameworked, murrine; soda-lime glass
PHOTO BY P. HULET

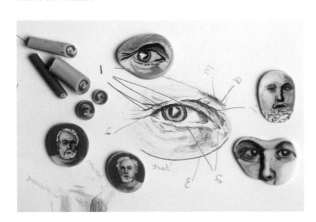

DINAH HULET
Jim's Wife, 2000
16 x 14 x 1½ inches (40.6 x 35.6 x 3.8 cm)
Flameworked, murrine; soda-lime glass
PHOTO BY P. HULET

SHARI MAXSON HOPPER
Textures, 1998
21½ inches (54.6 cm) long
Lampblown, kiln fired; enamel, borosilicate
glass tubing
PHOTO BY ARTIST

SHARI MAXSON HOPPER
Essential Elements, 2004
18 inches (45.7 cm) long
Lampblown, collaged, kiln fired, wound; enamel,
photos, borosilicate glass tubing, silk beads
PHOTOS BY ARTIST

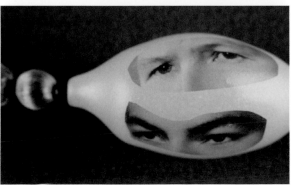

SHARI MAXSON HOPPER
Souvenirs, 1999
23 inches (58.4 cm) long
Lampblown, kiln fired; enamel, borosilicate glass tubing
PHOTO BY ARTIST

MATTHEW ESKUCHE
Hawaii Monos, 2005
26 x 14 x 10 inches (66 x 35.6 x 25.4 cm)
Flameworked; borosilicate glass
PHOTO BY ARTIST

MATTHEW ESKUCHE
16th Century 7-11, 2007
14 x 24 x 20 inches (35.6 x 61 x 50.8 cm)
Flameworked, mirrored; borosilicate glass
PHOTO BY DAVID SMITH

MATTHEW ESKUCHE
White Trash, 2007
16 x 58 x 20 inches (40.6 x 147.3 x 50.8 cm)
Flameworked; enamel, borosilicate glass
PHOTO BY DAVID SMITH

NATHAN R. PURCELL
African Throwing Knife I, 2007
14½ x 6 x 3 inches (36.8 x 15.2 x 7.6 cm)
Flameworked, sand carved, cold-worked; borosilicate glass
PHOTO BY ARTIST

NATHAN R. PURCELL
Zuri, 2007
15 x 7 x 7 inches (38.1 x 17.8 x 17.8 cm)
Flameworked, sandblasted, sand carved; borosilicate glass
PHOTO BY ARTIST

NATHAN R. PURCELL
Basket Series IV, V, 2007
19¼ x 9 x 3 inches (48.9 x 22.9 x 7.6 cm)
Flameworked, sand carved, sandblasted; glass, steel
PHOTO BY ARTIST

MARK PEISER
PWV 282 "Back Road, Fall Colors," 1980
9⅛ x 5⅛ inches (23.2 x 13 cm)
Blown, encased, torch worked; studio formulated zinc
potash crystal
PHOTO BY ANNE HAWTHORNE

MARK PEISER
PWV 198 "Swing at Horner Hall," 1979
6⅜ x 4⅜ inches (16.2 x 11.1 cm)
Blown, encased, torch worked; studio formulated
zinc potash crystal
PHOTO BY ANNE HAWTHORNE
COLLECTION OF PAUL STANKARD

MARK PEISER
PWV 250 "Telephone Pole," 1980
7¹¹⁄₁₆ x 4⅛ inches (19.5 x 10.5 cm)
Blown, encased, torch worked; studio formulated zinc
potash crystal
PHOTO BY ANNE HAWTHORNE

VICTOR CHIARIZIA
Untitled, 2002
22 x 7 inches (55.9 x 17.8 cm)
Blown, sand carved, acid etched, lampworked;
borosilicate glass, vitreous enamels
PHOTO BY ARTIST

MARK PEISER
PWV 335 "I Wonder What Happened to Patsy," 1981
9⅜ x 6 inches (23.8 x 15.2 cm)
Blown, encased, torch worked; studio formulated zinc
potash crystal
PHOTO BY ANNE HAWTHORNE

VICTOR CHIARIZIA
Choosing the Path, 2003
14 x 7 x 8 inches (35.6 x 17.8 x 20.3 cm)
Blown, crackled, sand carved, acid etched, lampworked;
soft glass, borosilicate glass, enamels
PHOTO BY ARTIST

DANIEL ADAMS
Untitled rings, 2001
1½ x 1 x ⅝ inches (3.8 x 2.5 x 1.6 cm)
Flameworked, cut; reduction frit, soda-lime
glass, silver by Chuck Domitrovich
PHOTO BY ROGER SCHREIBER

KATHRYN WARDILL
Branch Series Brooches, 2006–2007
1¹⁵⁄₁₆ x ¾ x ¾ inches (5 x 2 x 2 cm)
Lampworked; silver precious metal clay, glass, stainless steel
PHOTO BY ARTIST

KATHRYN WARDILL
Tall Bead Ring Series, 2001
Largest: 5⅞ x 1¹⁵⁄₁₆ x 1³⁄₁₆ inches (15 x 5 x 3 cm)
Hand carved, lost wax cast, flameworked; Bullseye glass
PHOTO BY ARTIST

KATHRYN WARDILL
Loose Glass Neckpiece Series, 2006–2007
11¾ x 5⅞ x 1¹⁵⁄₁₆ inches (30 x 15 x 5 cm)
Flameworked; glass, silver
PHOTO BY ARTIST

DANIEL ADAMS
Flora, 2007
Largest: 1½ inches (3.8 cm) in diameter
Flameworked, dots, cut, trail decorated, etched,
textured; frit, enamel, soda-lime glass, polymer
clay beads by Cynthia Toops
PHOTO BY ROGER SCHREIBER

DANIEL ADAMS
Jelly Bean, 2006
26 inches (66 cm) long
Flameworked, molded, engraved;
enamel, soda-lime glass
PHOTO BY ROGER SCHREIBER

DANIEL ADAMS
Snow in Seattle, 2001
18 inches (45.7 cm) long
Flameworked, cut; frit, enamel, soda-lime glass,
silver by Chuck Domitrovich
PHOTOS BY ROGER SCHREIBER

CARMEN LOZAR
Girl Honey, 2006
7 x 3½ x 4 inches (17.8 x 8.9 x 10.2 cm)
Flameworked, sandblasted, oil painted;
borosilicate glass
PHOTO BY VICTORIA PERELET
COURTESY OF D&A FINE ARTS/FOSTER WHITE GALLERY

CARMEN LOZAR
Sweet Sleep, 2006
3¼ x 5 x 4 inches (8.3 x 12.7 x 10.2 cm)
Flameworked, sandblasted, oil painted; borosilicate glass,
mixed media
PHOTO BY VICTORIA PERELET
COURTESY OF D&A FINE ARTS/FOSTER WHITE GALLERY

CARMEN LOZAR
Reliquary for My Everyday (The Garden), 2007
11½ x 8 inches (29.2 x 20.3 cm)
Flameworked, sandblasted, oil painted, blown; borosilicate
and soda-lime glasses, tomato
PHOTO BY VICTORIA PERELET
COURTESY OF D&A FINE ARTS/FOSTER WHITE GALLERY

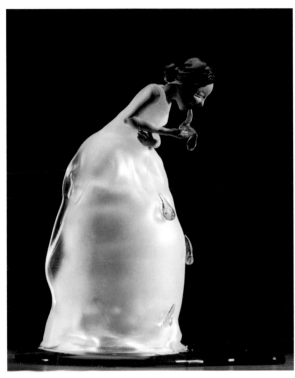

CARMEN LOZAR
Early Mourning, 2006
5 x 3½ x 4 inches (12.7 x 8.9 x 10.2 cm)
Flameworked, sandblasted, oil painted, constructed;
borosilicate glass, wood
PHOTO BY VICTORIA PERELET
COURTESY OF D&A FINE ARTS/FOSTER WHITE GALLERY

CARMEN LOZAR
Late One Nite the Hunter's Wife Was Found Out, 2005
12½ x 6½ x 5 inches (31.8 x 16.5 x 12.7 cm)
Flameworked, sandblasted, oil painted; borosilicate glass,
mixed media
PHOTO BY VICTORIA PERELET
COURTESY OF FOSTER WHITE GALLERY

CARMEN LOZAR
Bridge, 2004
7 x 6½ x 3½ inches (17.8 x 16.5 x 8.9 cm)
Flameworked, sandblasted, oil painted;
borosilicate glass, mixed media
PHOTO BY VICTORIA PERELET
COURTESY OF D&A FINE ARTS/FOSTER WHITE GALLERY

ALEX ARBELL
Untitled, 1991
12½ x 12 inches (31.8 x 30.5 cm)
Flameworked, blown; borosilicate glass,
metallic solutions, patina
PHOTO BY ARTIST

ALEX ARBELL
*Amphora with
Chained Stopper on
Metal Stand*, 1991
19 x 10½ inches
(48.3 x 26.7 cm)
Flameworked, blown;
borosilicate glass,
metallic solutions,
patina
PHOTO BY ARTIST

ALEX ARBELL
Amphora on Metal Stand, 1992
29 x 9½ x 13½ inches (73.7 x 24.1 x 34.3 cm)
Flameworked, blown; borosilicate glass, metallic
solutions, patina
PHOTO BY ARTIST

ALEX ARBELL
Amphora on Metal Stand, 1992
10 x 14 inches (25.4 x 35.6 cm)
Flameworked, blown; borosilicate glass, metallic solutions, patina
PHOTO BY ARTIST

RICHARD CLEMENTS
Golden Pillow Bottle, 2005
2¾ x 5¹⁵⁄₁₆ x 5¹⁵⁄₁₆ inches (7 x 15 x 15 cm)
Flameworked, sandblasted, fumed; borosilicate glass
PHOTO BY ARTIST

RICHARD CLEMENTS
Golden Urchin, 2004
11¾ x 3¹⁵⁄₁₆ x 11¾ inches (30 x 10 x 30 cm)
Flameworked, sandblasted, fumed; borosilicate glass
PHOTO BY ARTIST

RICHARD CLEMENTS
Bottles, 2007
5¹⁵⁄₁₆ x 2¾ inches (15 x 7 cm)
Flameworked; handmade colors, borosilicate glass
PHOTO BY ARTIST

RICHARD CLEMENTS
The Pillow Muncher, 2004
5½ x 4⅓ x 1⅔ inches (14 x 11 x 4 cm)
Flameworked, fumed; handmade colors, borosilicate glass
PHOTO BY ARTIST

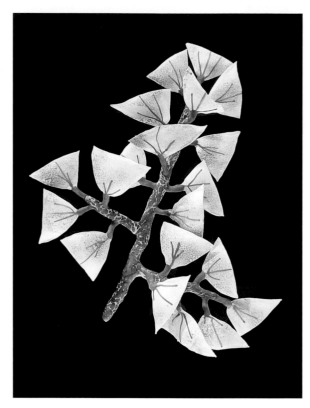

KATHLEEN ELLIOT
Remembering Dora's Hat, 2007
15 x 11 x 7 inches (38.1 x 27.9 x 17.8 cm)
Flameworked, blown, cut, assembled, sandblasted;
borosilicate glass
PHOTO BY KEAY EDWARDS

KATHLEEN ELLIOT
Botanica: Ripening Plums, 2006
14 x 8 x 4 inches (35.6 x 20.3 x 10.2 cm)
Flameworked, blown, cut, assembled, sandblasted;
borosilicate glass
PHOTO BY KEAY EDWARDS

KATHLEEN ELLIOT
Botanica: Four Pomegranates, 2007
18 x 14 x 6 inches (45.7 x 35.6 x 15.2 cm)
Flameworked, blown, cut, assembled, sandblasted;
borosilicate glass
PHOTO BY KEAY EDWARDS

KATHLEEN ELLIOT
Botanica: Yellow Nectarines, 2006
12 x 13 x 5 inches (30.5 x 33 x 12.7 cm)
Flameworked, blown, cut, assembled, sandblasted;
borosilicate glass
PHOTO BY KEAY EDWARDS

KATHLEEN ELLIOT
Botanica: Butterscotch Lantern Pods, 2005
12 x 15 x 5 inches (30.5 x 38.1 x 12.7 cm)
Flameworked, blown, cut, assembled,
sandblasted; borosilicate glass
PHOTOS BY KEAY EDWARDS

KATE FOWLE MELENEY
Green Hydra, 2004
2½ x ¾ x ¾ inches (6.4 x 1.9 x 1.9 cm)
Flameworked, etched, electroformed; soda-lime glass, silver leaf, copper leaf, copper, patina
PHOTO BY JERRY ANTHONY

KATE FOWLE MELENEY
Red Hydra, 2004
2 x 1 x 1 inches (5.1 x 2.5 x 2.5 cm)
Flameworked, electroformed; soda-lime glass, enamels, copper, patina
PHOTO BY JERRY ANTHONY

KATE FOWLE MELENEY
Filicea II, 2005
3 x ½ x ½ inches (7.6 x 1.3 x 1.3 cm)
Flameworked, electroformed; soda-lime glass, copper, patina
PHOTO BY JERRY ANTHONY

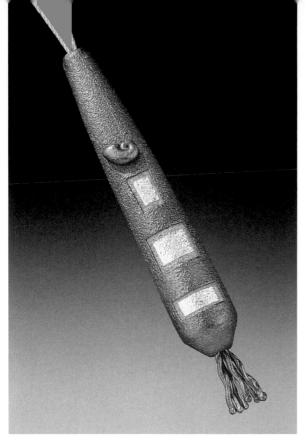

KATE FOWLE MELENEY
Neptune's Collage, 2004
3½ x ½ x ½ inches (8.9 x 1.3 x 1.3 cm)
Flameworked, appliqué, electroformed; soda lime glass,
enamel, gold foil, copper, patina
PHOTO BY JERRY ANTHONY

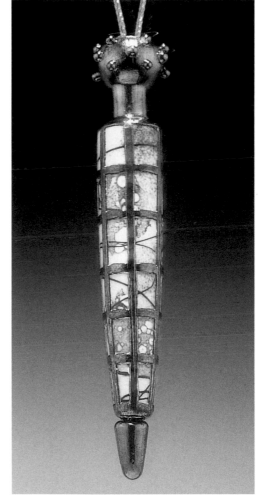

KATE FOWLE MELENEY
Anthropomorph II, 2004
3½ x ¾ x ¾ inches (8.9 x 1.9 x 1.9 cm)
Flameworked, electroformed; soda-lime glass, enamels,
copper leaf, copper, patina
PHOTO BY JERRY ANTHONY

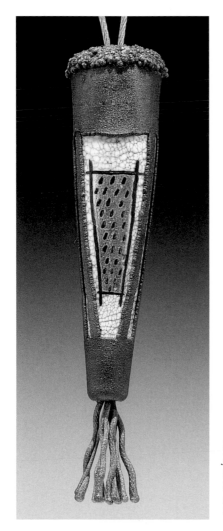

KATE FOWLE MELENEY
Japanese Trapezoid, 2003
3 x ¾ x ¾ inches (7.6 x 1.9 x 1.9 cm)
Flameworked, fumed, etched, electroformed, appliqué; soda-lime
glass, silver, copper, gold foil, ceramic overglazes, patina
PHOTO BY JERRY ANTHONY

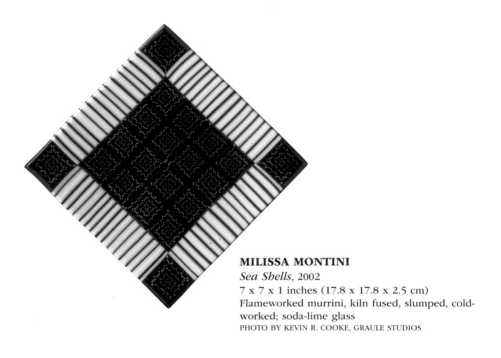

MILISSA MONTINI
Sea Shells, 2002
7 x 7 x 1 inches (17.8 x 17.8 x 2.5 cm)
Flameworked murrini, kiln fused, slumped, cold-worked; soda-lime glass
PHOTO BY KEVIN R. COOKE, GRAULE STUDIOS

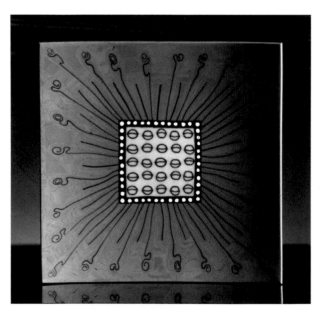

MILISSA MONTINI
Seeds, 2001
7 x 7 x 1 inches (17.8 x 17.8 x 2.5 cm)
Flameworked murrini, kiln fused, slumped,
cold-worked; soda-lime glass
PHOTO BY KEVIN R. COOKE, GRAULE STUDIOS

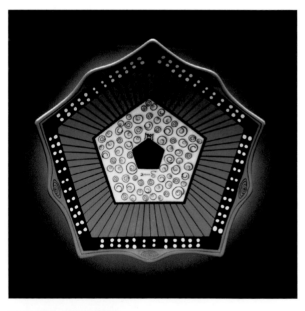

MILISSA MONTINI
Silvery Moon, 2006
8 x 2 inches (20.3 x 5.1 cm)
Flameworked murrini, kiln fused, slumped,
cold-worked; soda-lime glass
PHOTO BY KEVIN R. COOKE, GRAULE STUDIOS

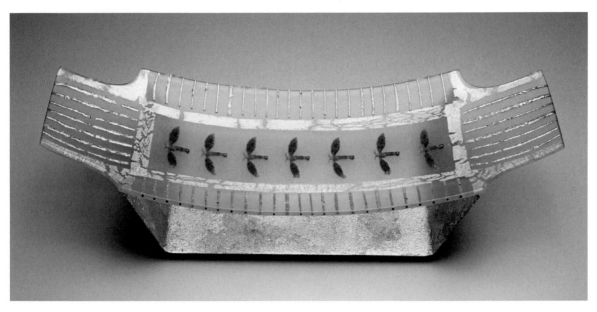

MILISSA MONTINI
Moth, 2005
10 x 3½ x 3 inches (25.4 x 8.9 x 7.6 cm)
Flameworked murrini, kiln fused, slumped, cold-worked;
soda-lime glass, brass and gold leaf stand, gold foil
PHOTO BY DAVID SMITH

MILISSA MONTINI
Flying Carpet, 2004
13 x 5 x 3 inches (33 x 12.7 x 7.6 cm)
Flameworked murrini, kiln fused, slumped, cold-worked;
soda-lime glass, brass stand, patina
PHOTO BY KEVIN R. COOKE, GRAULE STUDIOS

GINNY RUFFNER
The Cyclical Nature of Floral Fashion, 1999
13½ x 14 x 6 inches (34.3 x 35.6 x 15.2 cm)
Flameworked, sandblasted, painted;
borosilicate glass, acrylic paint
PHOTO BY MIKE SEIDL

GINNY RUFFNER
Brain Series: The Opulent Brain, 1996
18½ x 13 x 12½ inches (47 x 33 x 31.8 cm)
Flameworked, sandblasted, painted; borosilicate
glass, acrylic paint
PHOTO BY MIKE SEIDL

GINNY RUFFNER
Hummingbird's Ninth, 2005
16 x 12 x 8 inches (40.6 x 30.5 x 20.3 cm)
Flameworked, sandblasted, painted; borosilicate glass,
acrylic paint
PHOTO BY MIKE SEIDL

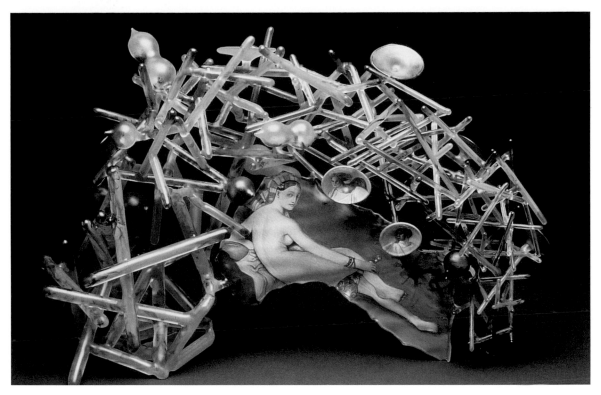

GINNY RUFFNER
Grand Oh, 1991
19 x 29 x 15 inches (48.3 x 73.7 x 38.1 cm)
Flameworked, sandblasted, painted; borosilicate
glass, acrylic paint
PHOTO BY MIKE SEIDL

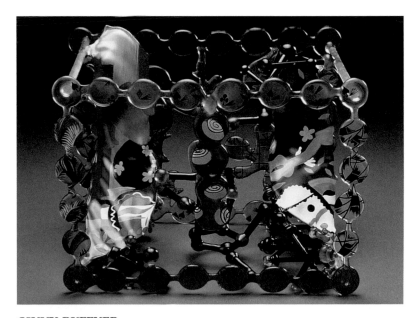

GINNY RUFFNER
Conceptual Narrative Series: What Is a Style, 1997
13 x 17½ x 12½ inches (33 x 44.5 x 31.8 cm)
Flameworked, sandblasted, painted; borosilicate glass,
acrylic paint
PHOTO BY MIKE SEIDL

Vittorio Costantini

Nature is the catalyst in the masterful work of Venetian flameworker Vittorio Costantini. Insects, fish, butterflies, and birds are among the creatures reproduced precisely in shape, color, and essence as Vittorio melts and manipulates glass. A faithful believer in the power of practice and patience at the torch, Vittorio lovingly describes the art of flamework as "incomparable and impossible to imitate."

Monarch Butterfly Life Cycle, 2001
Adult: 3⁷⁄₁₆ x 1⁹⁄₁₆ inches (8.8 x 4 cm)
Caterpillar: 2⅜ x ⅜ inches (6 x 1 cm)
Lampworked; soda-lime glass
PHOTO BY EVA HEYD
COURTESY OF MOSTLY GLASS GALLERY

The Natural

think I can still hear the voice of my mother calling me to get up and get ready for school. I really didn't like school. So, as soon as summer break began, my father—a fisherman who came from a family of fishermen—would take me along on his boat. I would help him pull in the nets and choose the fish. Sometimes we would fish in the sea or the lagoon, and once in a while we fished in the river. We also slept in the boat.

I enjoyed watching the birds as they followed us in our boat. When we would stop to meet some farmers to exchange our fish for milk or cheese, I loved to observe all the animals in the farmyards and the insects that were found in the fields.

Then, for a brief period, I worked for very little pay in a *squero*, where fishing boats are built. I also worked for a small metal shop, where we made nails. I was immediately fascinated with the fire and the fact that it could melt iron. Unfortunately, the metal shop closed after just one year.

I was eleven years old when I began working as a *garzonetto*—an assistant—at a furnace in a factory in Murano. Every morning, my mother would call out to me to go catch the boat to Burano that would take me to Murano. The children who worked in the glass factories were treated like slaves, due to a few ignorant maestros.

For several years I worked my way up in different factories. At that time, during the 1950s and 1960s, it was impossible to become a maestro unless you were of Muranese origin.

Birds, 2006–2007
Largest: 5⅞ x 1⁹⁄₁₆ inches (15 x 4 cm)
Flameworked; soda-lime glass
PHOTO BY GIAN MAURO LAPENNA

Vittorio Costantini

School of Tropical Fish, 1999
19¹¹⁄₁₆ inches (50 cm)
Lampworked; soda-lime glass
PHOTO BY GIAN MAURO LAPENNA

Over the years and thanks to my capability, my situation changed. I became very respected and had no problem finding a job. However, there were still many difficult years in Murano, due to strikes and protests that resulted from the Italian employment crisis.

At age nineteen, I bought my first torch on sale. I wanted to learn to work *a lume*—flameworking—so that I could have an alternative job just in case my factory closed. One day, a friend introduced me to a master glassblower who, in his free time, did flameworking. The master asked me to reproduce an animal figure that he had been making for several years. I gave it my best effort. Sometime later, my friend told me that the master had said I had no talent whatsoever and would never have a future in flameworking!

I continued to work in a factory, and in the evenings I practiced flameworking to better my skills. My first laboratory was in a tiny room on the island of Burano. I arranged my furnishings: a small table, a chair, and my torch. The first pieces that I created were a fly and an ant. I bought a small book that illustrated the particularities of these insects, and my strong attraction to nature surely helped me a great deal.

THE BIG JUMP

Because working in the factory did not satisfy me fully, and above all because holding this job meant I was not free to realize my dreams, I decided to abandon my job and dedicate myself solely to flameworking. In 1974 I opened my laboratory in Venice. During the years I worked in factories, I had to produce objects designed and ordered by others, but now I was finally free to experiment with my own talents and realize something completely of my own making.

The big turnaround in my life happened when I was invited to participate in two important exhibitions in Venice, in 1981 and 1982. These exhibitions brought national and international attention to my work. They also pushed me to improve my technique and to try to create more complicated pieces—sometimes to the point at which the work was impossible to realize.

I think the experience I had and technique I learned in the factories helped me a lot with flameworking. During the years that followed, and as my experience deepened, I perfected the techniques—filigree, the application of gold and silver leaf, millefiori, and more—that have allowed me to recreate objects that are very detailed in both shape and color. It is incredible to me, still, that

Vittorio Costantini

there is something new to learn every day, such as a simple move with the pinchers or the choice of one color over another.

To find the perfect form and appropriate proportion for every piece, I employ a study of each one that can take up to one week to create, as well as innumerable tests, perhaps using just one color. Then I do still more experiments to find the most realistic colors possible.

Inspiration is very important in my work. Without inspiration, making nice objects is still possible, thanks to technique and my years of experience, but for me, the object must transmit some kind of sensation and emotion. For this reason, I love to watch nature documentaries and do a lot of research in books. I have a fine collection of books, most of it given to me by

friends and as gifts from glass collectors. Wherever I visit, if there is an aquarium or a botanical garden, I absolutely must go see it! I enjoy having contact with nature and, whenever possible, observing animals in their natural habitats or protected environments.

During my sojourn as an instructor at Penland School of Crafts in Penland, North Carolina, I woke up early every morning and walked around the grounds. I saw butterflies, insects, and birds. By the time class started, I had already had an infusion of energy and the stimulation to recreate some of these species in demonstrations for the students.

Every day provides challenges for me. Perhaps this is true because of my stubborn character. I am never satisfied with the first pieces I make. I am meticulous in reproducing every detail. The first thing I do each morning in my laboratory is skim through some books and look at the designs and photographs for inspiration.

When I'm asked what my favorite piece is, I always respond that it is the one I'll be working on tomorrow. This is my great challenge: to continue to move forward and create pieces that are even more complicated and difficult to duplicate.

FLAMEWORKING MASTERS AND BEGINNERS

Flameworking has received appropriate recognition only in the past few decades, thanks to the efforts of people I consider to be glass artisans. The quality of the objects and the creativity of these artisans have triggered the evolution of flame-working, so much so that this subject is now taught in the finest schools around the world. Flameworking has succeeded in growing up from—

Mantis Shrimp, 2002
$6^{11}/_{16}$ x $1^{15}/_{16}$ inches (17 x 5 cm)
Flameworked; soda-lime glass
PHOTO BY GIAN MAURO LAPENNA

Hermit Crab & Murex Brandaris, 2007
Hermit crab: 3⅛ x 2⅜ inches (8 x 6 cm)
Murex: 2¾ x 1⁹/₁₆ inches (7 x 4 cm)
Flameworked; soda-lime glass
PHOTO BY GIAN MAURO LAPENNA

Vittorio Costantini

Lagoon of Venice, 2005
Largest: 3⁹⁄₁₆ x 2⅜ inches (9 x 6 cm)
Lampworked; soda-lime glass
PHOTO BY FRANCESCO FERRUZZI

Wasp Hive, 2003
Wasp hive:
9¹³⁄₁₆ x 7⅞ inches
(25 x 20 cm)
Wasp: 1 x 1 inch
(2.5 x 2.5 cm)
Lampworked;
soda-lime glass
PHOTO BY EVA HEYD
COURTESY OF MOSTLY
GLASS GALLERY

Insects, 2006–2007
Largest: 3⅛ x 1⁹⁄₁₆ inches (8 x 4 cm)
Flameworked; soda-lime glass
PHOTO BY GIAN MAURO LAPENNA

Vittorio Costantini

or separating out from—the stereotypical concept that equates flameworked objects with souvenirs for tourists, which in turn equates to "cheap stuff."

Among the glass artisans I respect highly are the following:

Lucio Bubacco. We first met in 1983 during a cultural exhibit in Venice, where we both displayed our works. More than 20 years later, we met again at the glass workshops on the island of San Servolo in Venice. I began frequenting Lucio's studio, to give demonstrations to his students, to discuss our projects and experiences, and to exchange advice— as well as just to visit together. Lucio's fervent imagination, energy, and wonderful craftsmanship enable him to create unique works of his own genre. His studio, rich with human anatomy, transforms glass into a harmonious sculpture, a mythical inspiration, and a contemporary art form.

Dinah Hulet. Sometimes it happens that we meet people for the first time and feel that we've always known them. This happened when I met Dinah. Right away, I was impressed by her sweetness and honesty. I admired her passion and dedication to researching the technique of *murrine*. When I met up with her again, I could see the continuous evolutions that have allowed her to create incredible *murrine* on the torch.

Marshall Hyde. Marshall is an American who was a young man when he and his wife visited my laboratory years ago. Years later, he became my first student at The Studio of The Corning Museum of Glass in Corning, New York, and he eventually became my assistant at the Pilchuck School of Glass in Stanwood, Washington. I admire Marshall—whom I call Marcello—for his spirited personality, his generosity, his accessibility, and his persistence. He is a true glass sculptor whose innate talent illustrates his wonderful creativity and imagination.

Loren Stump. I've long admired the works of Loren Stump. I was especially fascinated by his sculptures—both by their dimensions and their perfect detailing. I wondered how these qualities were possible with the technique of flameworking. When I finally met him in 2001, at the Glass Art Society Conference in Corning, New York, I learned that this nice, humorous man is a creative genius who offers volcanic ideas and energy.

Cesare Toffolo. I first admired the goblets—handblown using borosilicate glass—of this master lampworker. He succeeds in creating unique objects that demonstrate an uncommon ability and bravura. Cesare founded Centro Studio Vetro, a nonprofit association that organizes glass workshops on the island of San Servolo in Venice and that attracts great masters from Murano, as well as internationally. Cesare convinced me to participate as an instructor for one of these workshops, and I must thank him: Teaching was a great and enriching experience.

MY TEACHING PHILOSOPHY

As a teacher, I stress that people who are attracted to flameworking for the first time must be armed with patience and diligence, and, above all, they must possess a passion for this approach to glass, which is incomparable and impossible to imitate.

Do not be discouraged if your first pieces break. It is very important to remember that learning flameworking takes a lot of time. Never surrender when faced with difficulty or an obstacle.

For me, the choice of glass is important, as is the choice of various tools, including the torch, tweezers, and scissors. The work table must be organized in such a way that you can easily find whatever you need—for example, glass rods, tools, or a sketch, design, or photograph of what you want to recreate.

When you read the Hands On section that follows, you will see numerous techniques that are easily applied with just a bit of experience. Remember that it is important to keep the glass hot, especially the area where more hot glass is added. To do this, a certain amount of manual skill is necessary.

Like so much in flameworking, this skill can only be acquired through extensive practice. You must try over and over again.

Hands On

Vittorio Costantini demonstrates how to make a fish, including the application of silver foil and the creation of a filigrana *lattice.*

1   When choosing a fish to make, I am often inspired by books. I choose the glass rods—in transparent and opaque colors—that I'll need, and I gather all the necessary tools, such as tweezers, a butter knife, and pinchers. I also cut and set aside silver foil, which will be needed later.

2   To create stringers, which will be applied later to create the *filigrana*—the white lattice portion of the fish—I first gather a small ball of glass at one end of a white, opaque rod. I repeat this process with a black, opaque rod; the resulting stringers will be used to make the fish's eyes.

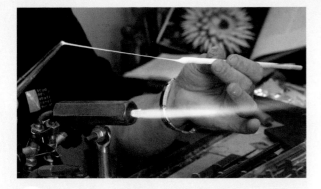

3   When the small glass ball is hot, I pull it, using tweezers, to make the thin stringer.

4   I heat up one end of a clear glass rod. I shape that end into a ball and then start to shape the ball into a cylinder.

5   I shape the ball of clear glass into a cylinder by rolling it on a graphite paddle.

6   Using one of the white stringers that I made earlier (in the photo, I'm holding it in my right hand), I apply a white stripe to the cylinder, from the top to the bottom. Next, I reheat the entire cylinder, slowly turning the glass in the flame. I then use the white stringer to apply similar stripes all around the cylinder, leaving small spaces between them and reheating the cylinder after every application.

7   Using my right hand, I take a clear glass rod and heat the top of it.

8   When the glass rod is heated, I attach it to the end of the cylinder.

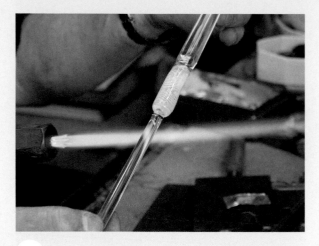

9 Slowly, I twist both glass rods in the flame. I achieve a lattice effect on the cylinder by twisting and turning the glass.

10 I heat the *filigrana* cylinder again, and then ...

11 ... I detach the glass rod from the cylinder.

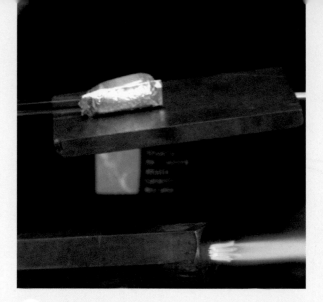

12 I place the fish base on top of a piece of silver foil. I press the foil onto the fish base by rolling the base over it. Only half of the piece is covered with the foil. I then reheat the piece completely.

13 Using heated transparent rods of various colors, I apply colored stripes, one next to another, to the foil-covered area of the base. I reheat the base after each application.

14 After placing the base on a graphite paddle, I press down lightly with another graphite paddle to flatten the top and the bottom. The piece is then heated again.

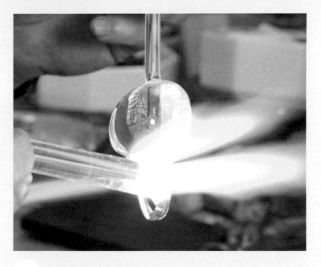

15 To form the central part of the fishbone, I use the black stringer that I made earlier to apply a stripe between the *filigrana* application and the silver foil. I heat the piece again, and place the fish base in the kiln, detaching the glass rod.

16 I prepare a punty (or handle) by heating a transparent rod.

17 I reach into the kiln and attach the hot punty to the fish base, making sure the silver-foil section is oriented face up. Then I heat the piece again.

18 With my other hand, I heat a quantity of clear glass, and then use it to completely cover both flat sides of the fish base. The piece is then reheated.

19 To create the desired form of the fish, I use tweezers to stretch the fish base lightly, and then I reheat it.

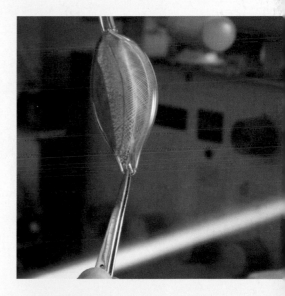

20 The gills are created using an ordinary butter knife, which I press lightly into the hot glass. I reheat the piece again.

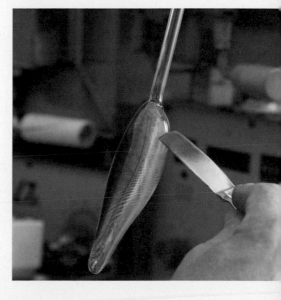

21 To make the fish's eyes, first I apply dots with a heated white stringer. Then I use a black stringer to apply black dots on top of the white ones. The piece is reheated.

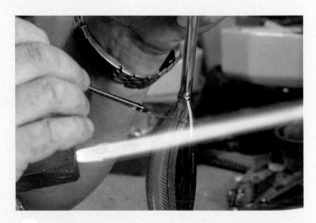

22 I cover the eyes by melting transparent glass on top of them.

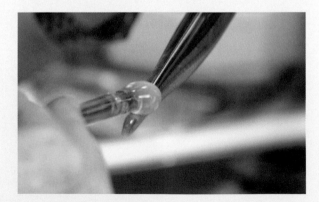

23 To create the fish's tail, I form a ball at one end of a heated rod of transparent glass and attach the ball to the tail area of the fish body. I heat the piece again.

24 The basic tail shape is made with a mini squasher and then refined by squeezing and pulling the glass with tweezers.

25 To create the fish's various fins and their desired textures and shapes, I repeat the processes in steps 23 and 24, attaching balls of glass, flattening them with a mini squasher and squeezing and pulling them with tweezers. I then reheat the entire fish completely.

26 I detach the mouth end of the fish from the glass punty by grabbing the tail with pinchers and lightly pulling the mouth end away from the rod, which is being heated by the flame. While still holding the fish tail, I use a butter knife to create the fish's mouth.

27 I carefully place the fish in the kiln to anneal and complete the piece.

About the Artist

Vittorio Costantini was born in 1944 on the island of Burano, which is near Murano and situated in the lagoon of Venice, Italy. Like many islanders, he is the son of a fisherman. His mother was a lacemaker.

Vittorio began an apprenticeship in a glass factory at age eleven. Initially, lampworking was a hobby that occupied the little time he had after a long day working in the factory.

Since he opened his own workshop in Venice, flameworking has become his one and only focus and passion. Vittorio says he has always had an innate fascination with nature, and all his creations evidence not just a mastery of his art but also his love of nature. He spends countless hours creating individual pieces—multicolored insects, iridescent butterflies, birds, fish, and colorful flowers—that reflect this devotion.

Vittorio considers himself to be a great observer of the "little universe"—the microcosmos—that surrounds human beings daily. With the profound vision of an artist, he sees deep into the fields, skies, and waters to observe what many people easily overlook.

Vittorio has participated in numerous exhibitions in Italy and abroad. His work has been shown in museums around the world, including Palazzo Grassi and Palazzo Ducale in Venice; the Museum of Natural History in Bologna, Italy; the Museum of Venetian Art in Otaru, Japan; the Oceanographic Museum in Monaco-Ville, Monaco; and The Corning Museum of Glass in Corning, New York. He is committed to developing knowledge about flameworking and, in recent years, has enjoyed devoting himself to teaching and demonstrating.

People who visit his laboratory in Venice can admire his rich personal collection. This collection of pieces is a testimony to his many years of flameworking and the evolution of his technique.

Gaudy Sea Anemone with Skunk Clownfish, 2002
8⅝ x 7⁷⁄₁₆ x 5⅞ inches (22 x 18 x 15 cm)
Lampworked; soda-lime glass
PHOTO BY GIAN MAURO LAPENNA

Sally Prasch

Scientific and artistic approaches to glass
are melded in the spirited flamework of Sally
Prasch. Trained in scientific glassblowing,
fine arts, and applied science, Sally explores
the outer limits of glass art in her subject
matter, even as she tests the boundaries of the
material itself. She uses the lathe extensively
and advocates for its creative possibilities
for flameworkers.

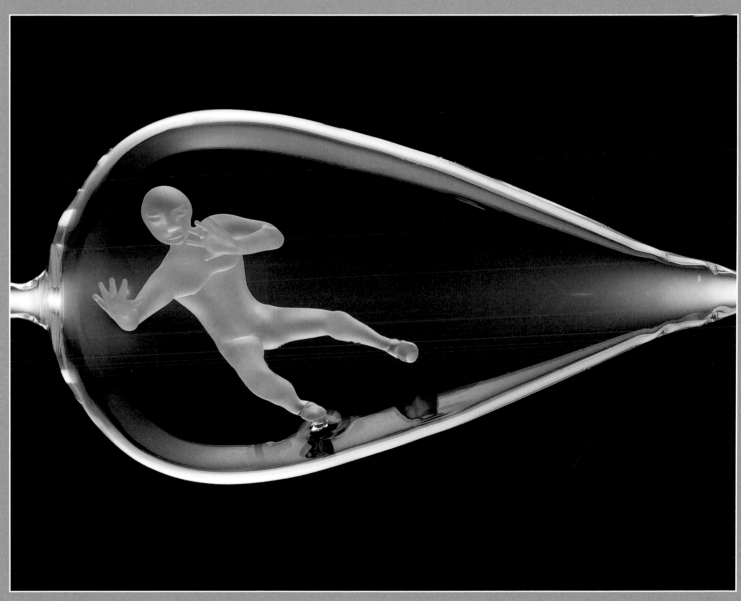

Pushing Light, 1994
7 x 12 x 7 inches (17.8 x 30.5 x 17.8 cm)
Flameworked, lathed, benched; neon
PHOTO BY TOMMY ELDER

I recall my father telling me, not long before his death, that I was the most normal kid he had. As a woman in my fifties, I still think I am just an average gal. There is nothing spectacular or outstanding about me—except for my talents in glass and science.

Working with glass mesmerizes me. It sucks me in as if it were a campfire. Just as you can gaze at a campfire's embers and flames for an entire evening, I can—and will—watch glass melt for a lifetime. When I work glass, depending on the shape that I am creating, the fire changes along with the mood of the piece and myself, and something new emerges.

I believe that, for good or for bad, we are molded by our families. I was fortunate to have a broadly supportive family. Both of my parents had teaching backgrounds, and they wanted to open up the world to their children. My parents, my brother (a professor of history), and my sister (a social worker) helped me form who I am. I am not saying we were happy all the time, but we did learn from each other, and we are still doing so.

When my siblings and I were young, my father planned summer family vacations. These explorations usually included visiting some of the many wonders located throughout the United States—the World's Fair in New York City, the Statue of Liberty, Beatnik Square, the Grand Canyon, Chinatown in San Francisco, the Redwood Forest, Yellowstone, and many more. My father took me to the musicals *Hair* and *Tommy* to open my mind even more.

We often spent holidays with my cousins, and over the years I watched how our family evolved. I experienced the full cycle of family life—family members getting old or sick and passing on, the birth of younger generations, children growing and maturing. All that I could see, feel, hear, smell, and taste of my experiences at home and in the world is in me now. And all of what is in me seeps into my work.

I was very fortunate to fall into working with glass. I was at the right place at the right time. Any medium might have worked, but almost by accident, glass was placed in front of me by Lloyd Moore, one of the best teachers on earth.

I was born in California, and my family moved around until we settled in Nebraska. I remember that when my father told the family he had accepted a job in Lincoln, Nebraska, my first thought was that I should know where Lincoln was. Although I had learned geography in school, I had no idea, really, and moving from Minnesota's Twin Cities to Lincoln was a bit of a shock. My father had accepted a job as the superintendent of public schools. My mother, who had given up teaching when she married my father, took up the stock market. (In those days, if two teachers who taught in the same

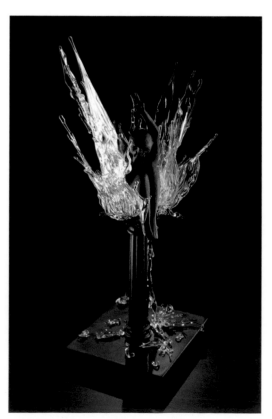

Jump into Peace, 2007
22 x 10 x 10 inches (55.9 x 25.4 x 25.4 cm)
Flameworked; borosilicate glass, cast bronze
PHOTO BY TOMMY ELDER

district got married, one of them had to give up teaching.) Both of my parents could see that I was struggling with the move to Nebraska and with school. My mother probably thought I was going to run away.

To keep me busy, my mother signed up me and my sister for a few classes at our local YMCA. One of the classes I took was with Lloyd Moore, who was the scientific glassblower at the University of Nebraska. I found that I loved working with glass, and it wasn't long before I was helping Lloyd teach beginner classes. I also worked with Lloyd at craft shows on weekends. My career in glass had begun.

LIFE LESSONS IN GLASS

Working Nebraska craft shows with Lloyd, in the early 1970s, taught me a lot about people and their prejudices. Sometimes we would go to very small towns. Television was the only place where some locals had ever seen a black person, so seeing Lloyd—an older black man—with a younger white woman was not an everyday occurrence, and people stared. I have to admit that on some days, I found myself a little concerned.

We would set up outside in the bright, hot sun, while people stood back and watched from a distance. After lighting two torches, Lloyd, in his radio voice, would announce, "We can make anything out of glass. Just ask, and we will make whatever you want." On the table for viewing and sale were the typical glass novelties—mixed with glass slaves holding up their chained arms. Swaying in the wind were glass scales depicting political events of the day and motorcycles that had moving glass wheels. All of our glass human figures had Afros. When a big motorcycle guy with long, straight hair asked Lloyd to "make me," I remember Lloyd looking at me over his glasses and telling the gentleman that Sally would be much better at creating him. I found that learning on the spot was a great challenge, but I did indeed learn how to make straight hair. Lloyd would always have a crowd gathered around us by the end of the day, and we would all be having a great time.

Working craft shows was a fantastic education, and teaching glass has always inspired me as well. I started teaching even before I could get paid. Most of the time, I was teaching adults. I practiced

Sally Prasch

Don't Touch This, 1996
9 inches (22.9 cm) in diameter
Flameworked; borosilicate glass
PHOTO BY TOMMY ELDER

Splash, 2003
13 x 13 x 13 inches (33 x 33 x 33 cm)
Flameworked, lathed, benched; borosilicate glass
PHOTO BY TOMMY ELDER

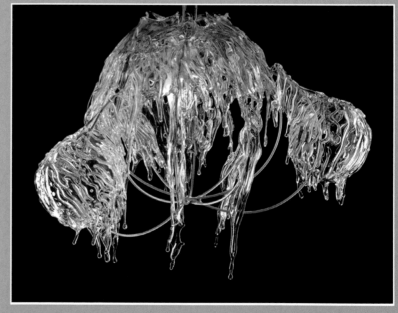

H_2O Light, 2007
10 x 15 x 10 inches (25.4 x 38.1 x 25.4 cm)
Flameworked, heat and gravity shaped, textured, etched; soda-lime glass,
borosilicate glass, applied dichroic coating, wielded steel
PHOTO BY TOMMY ELDER

Sally Prasch

Shattered Shell, 1994
Life size
Flameworked; borosilicate glass
PHOTO BY TOMMY ELDER

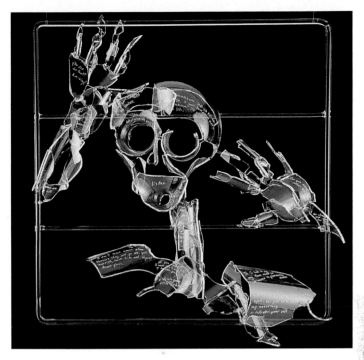

Listen, 1993
18 x 18 x 18 inches (45.7 x 45.7 x 45.7 cm)
Flameworked, engraved; borosilicate glass
PHOTO BY TOMMY ELDER

every technique diligently. My parents let me set up my own little torch in the basement so I could repeat techniques over and over again.

I worked with Lloyd from junior high through high school, learning about much more than glass. I would watch Lloyd teach and try to teach like him. Lloyd would assign challenging projects that not only taught technique but also made students realize that they had to keep their cool and not freak out. If you don't keep steady, nothing will work.

Lloyd's positive attitude in teaching carried over to me. I also had to learn to read people so they would open up to me as a teacher, as they did to Lloyd. What are you about? Why are you learning to work glass? Is it really glass that you want to learn about? By teaching and watching others teach, I learned about the energy between people—both between teacher and student and in the group dynamic. That energy, which can be found in any good class, stems from the trust between people and the willingness to learn and teach.

My parents always encouraged my studies in glass. I was diagnosed with dyslexia in the first grade. In those days, students with learning disabilities were encouraged to learn a skill. My mother once told me that our doctor had said some

students with dyslexia were unable to finish high school. She also said, "Ford and Einstein both had dyslexia, and look how they turned out."

My feeling about dyslexia is that it lets me look at things as a whole, rather than as individual parts or groups. When I memorized the periodic table, for example, I looked at it as a whole—a single thing with patterns and shapes. The table made sense to me in that way. I understood why the elements fit together, while other students, who used flash cards, had a hard time understanding the way things interacted. In fact, I think people with dyslexia have a great advantage in studying science. Of course, I was determined to prove my doctor wrong about people with dyslexia having a hard time finishing school. So, now I have three degrees—in fine arts, applied science, and scientific glass technology. I continue taking classes even today but feel that I cannot finance any more degrees!

In the early 1970s, most colleges did not offer glass classes. After doing some college work in Nebraska, I started school at the University of Kansas, where I could get a degree in ceramics while specializing in glass.

Sally Prasch

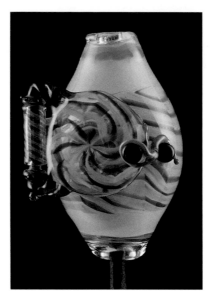

Flower Power Fountain, 1999
17 x 12 x 12 inches (43.2 x 30.5 x 30.5 cm)
Flameworked, slumped, fused; borosilicate glass
PHOTO BY TOMMY ELDER

Open to Peace, 2002
1 inch (2.5 cm)
Flameworked; borosilicate glass
PHOTO BY TOMMY ELDER

Until then, I hadn't realized that being a woman working in glass was different from being a man. I found myself in a glass class with very vocal men and one other woman. My professor told me he was not going to waste time teaching a woman, because I was just going to go off and get married and pregnant and forget about glass. That professor apologized 10 years later.

There wasn't much support for women in glass at that time, but I was lucky to have a great graduate student teacher, Craig Holt, who helped me through. I also was lucky to attend classes taught by glass artists such as Ray Schultz, William Bernstein, Lino Tagliapietra, Finn Lingaard, Carl Powell, Harold Gross, and Cesare Toffolo. Watching these people work glass excited and inspired me. Attending Glass Art Society and American Scientific Glassblowers Society conferences introduced me to many wonderful glass workers, including Sylvia Vigiletti (who in the early days let students sneak in free); Audrey Handler; Mary White; Beth Hylen; and Gerhard Finkenbeiner. Working with and learning from other glass artists continue to motivate me in my glass work.

During my first year out of college, I split my time between working for a furnace glassblower and working with Lloyd in the chemistry department at the University of Nebraska. Doing both proved to be too much, so I chose to work with Lloyd and start my own business on the side. I later moved my glass business to Massachusetts and continued my work in both artistic and scientific glassblowing.

When I started to receive an increasing number of requests for the fabrication of fused quartz apparatus, I felt I needed more training, so I went back to school and received degrees in scientific glass technology and applied science. I have since worked as a scientific glassblower for AT&T, the University of Massachusetts, the University of Vermont, Syracuse University, and various technical businesses. I thought the glass art world was male-dominated, but I found the field of scientific glassblowing to be even more so. The American Scientific Glassblowers Society has about 600 men and four women. There are many reasons for this bias, but that discussion could form a whole book chapter by itself!

Sally Prasch

A SCIENTIFIC APPROACH TO ART

I love science, and I love art. I do not see much difference between being a scientist and being an artist. Both artists and scientists are reaching for something unknown that they see in their minds. Both are creating. Both are fussy in that they know exactly what they want to achieve.

For some reason, just as furnace glassworkers do not want to mingle with flameworkers, artists and scientists rarely come together. When I am in the science world, people refer to me as the glassblower who does a little art. In the art-glass world, I am the artist who does a little scientific glassblowing.

To be honest, I cannot do one without the other. What I have learned as a scientific glassblower enables me to be proficient at glass lathe work and gives me the ability to create whatever I want to within millimeter accuracy. What I have learned in my art classes expands my capabilities in scientific work. Without any preconceived ideas about what can be done in glass, scientists come up with the wildest designs that challenge and change me. I believe that science is helping the world, and I want to be a part of that movement.

I have always thought it unfortunate that people label different styles of working with glass. Hot glass, flat glass, warm glass—it's all glass to me. Categorizing just separates people and limits them.

Lathe-working techniques play important roles in my work. I look at the lathe as just another glass tool—one that greatly expands the possibilities of what can be done in flameworking.

Most scientific glassblowing shops have lathes to enable glass workers to fabricate products for scientists. These machines help scientific glassblowers make very precise apparatus, whether large or small, thick or thin. They hold and rotate your glass, so you can have both hands free to work torches, or just sit back and think. The largest-diameter piece of glass I have worked in the lathe, for a quartz bell jar, was 3 feet (91.4 cm); the longest was a 15-foot (4.6 m) diffusion tube. Without a lathe, I could not have worked these pieces. I find that the lathe offers infinite creative possibilities to glass artists.

Glassblowing lathes have been used in America since 1924. They were first used in the vacuum-tube industry. I highly recommend that glass artists visit a scientific glassblowing shop to see how scientific glassblowers work on these machines. I have seen some really big lathes—and the different torches that go with them—in the glass industries. Most industries have refined the process of making glass items so that prices stay low. Instead of reinventing the wheel, take a look at what has been done already. Industry makes some of the largest and smallest glass items, and we all can learn from how industry works glass.

When working with a lathe, you must always think about safety. Wear protective clothing. The lathe is a machine; it will not stop if you get in its way, so know where you are in relation to your work. Know where your hands are, and do not let them or anything else get caught in the lathe. Think before touching. Could things be too hot or too sharp? Move slowly, and with care and thought.

With flameworking in general, before you begin you should plan how to set things up and how you are going to go through the steps of making what you plan to make, from start to finish. Use your resources properly. Use the right fire for the job. Heat only the glass you need by keeping most of the heat on a specific area. Throwing big flames around may look really cool, but I find it wasteful and dangerous. Try to think of all the things that could go wrong, and have a backup plan ready.

The extensive time that I have spent working with glass has allowed me to become very comfortable with it. I enjoy working with other mediums, such as clay and metal, but so far I am not as at ease with them as I am with glass. But even though I am most comfortable with glass, my work is not about glass or what I make with glass. It is about the emotional space surrounding me when I am creating. My work tells a story.

Back when I had worked with glass for 20 years, I thought I knew a lot. I believed I had all the time in the world to create whatever my heart desired. Now, as I reach 37 years of working with this medium, I simply don't know where to find the time to learn and make everything that I would like to.

I have so many stories to tell.

Sally Prasch

Hands On

Sally Prasch demonstrates scientific techniques, including the use of a lathe, as she creates a flower in a drop.

This piece was inspired by one of the many stories my mother used to tell my family; it was about the Dust Bowl storms of the 1930s and how Franklin Delano Roosevelt was the first president to talk about the conservation of our natural resources—water being one of them. I always find it fascinating that glass can look so much like water. The flower cannot exist without water, because nothing living can exist without water.

I am creating this piece for my mother, who didn't like to dust tiny, fragile things. The drop surrounding the flower would have made this piece easier for my mother to dust.

1 Among the tools I frequently use are my lathe, …

2 … cradle burners, which I use to heat larger tubing, …

3 … hand torches (here are two, but I have many more to fit whatever job I'm doing), …

4 … and multi stoppers.

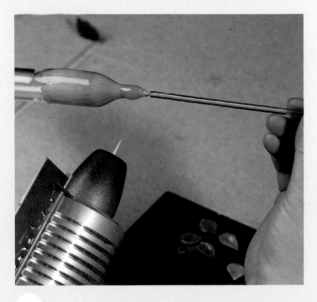

5 I start by making the petals of the flower at the bench torch. I mix colors of glass and layer them onto a tube. Then, by blowing and forming, I create the petal shape I desire.

6 I rip the side open with a cold piece of glass.

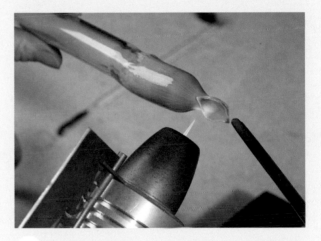

7 Using gravity as an ally, I let the petal open.

8 I create all my petals before assembling the flower.

Sally Prasch

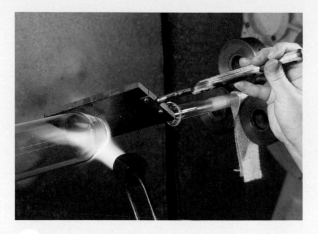

9 Now working on the lathe, I shape two tubes, which I will fuse together in a straight seal.

10 Keeping the heat on one area, the straight seal between the two tubes is completed.

11 Using heat, gravity, air, and graphite tools, I shape the larger tube to create the base of what will be the drop. I've set up a multi stopper, straight swivel, and blow hose into the end of the

large tube that is positioned in the chuck of the lathe's headstock. This allows me to expand the heated tube, blowing it into the desired drop shape.

12 The tools I use to shape the glass are graphite rods and paddles. It's important not to heat the graphite too much, or the lives of the tools will be shortened.

13 I measure parts of the flower, which I made up in full ahead of time, to make sure they will fit in the drop. All these parts are sealed onto glass rods, which serve as handles that give me control when I place the parts into the piece.

Sally Prasch

14 I take off the tube I've been using as a handle and remove some of the excess glass left behind.

15 To finish the base of the drop, I use a graphite paddle to flatten the area that will represent the water. This piece is then taken out of the lathe, so the top of the drop can be made.

16 The setup and process for starting the bubble for the top of the drop are the same as the ones I used to make the base. Instead of shaping the glass with tools, though, I use a large, bushy flame to create a taper on the top.

17 Employing a small flame positioned closely under the tube, I pull out the tailstock of the lathe until the glass opens and the bubble separates from the tube. This technique, which is called fire cutting, leaves a clean edge for sealing. After making a fire cut, it's important to heat both tubes so that no thin, sharp edges are left.

18 Using a graphite rod, I shape the opening of the bottom of the drop so that it's the same size as the top of the base.

19 I've placed the base of the drop back into the chuck of the lathe's headstock. I slowly bring it up to a working temperature.

Sally Prasch

20 The stem for the flower is attached. I insert it through the base tube, seal it to the inner flattened surface of the glass, and break off the punty.

21 The multi stopper, straight swivel, and blow hose are all in place and ready to use at this point. The leaf has already been sealed on hot, and the rod then removed with a small flame. The leaf's seals are worked in well here.

22 The flower is attached, and the glass rod holding it is melted off.

23 I go over the seals with the flame one more time to make sure there aren't any cold ones. Then I create a small hole in the surface of the glass, under the flower. In the next step, this hole will enable me to blow air into both the base and the top of the vessel.

24 I move the lathe's tailstock, with the top of the drop in it, until the rim of the top is aligned with the flattened surface of the base in the chuck of the headstock. By heating the edges of each piece so they're soupy hot, the blind seal is easy to accomplish. While the glass is hot, I blow through the base to keep the shapes of both the bottom and the top of the drop.

25 I'm careful to work the seal out well. I do not want any sharp edges.

Sally Prasch

26 After fire cutting the tube on the base to remove it, I heat the base and paddle its bottom end flat. The top is heated and the excess glass pulled straight off to create a pointed end, and the glass is placed in the annealing oven.

About the Artist

Sally Prasch started working in glass in 1970, with Lloyd Moore. She received her bachelor of fine arts degree from the University of Kansas and degrees in applied science and scientific glass technology from Salem Community College in Carney's Point, New Jersey. Holding the belief that one learns while teaching and sharing, Sally has embraced the central role of teaching in her life and in her own ongoing education. The schools at which she has taught include Pilchuck Glass School in Stanwood,

Baby, 1998
9 x 4 x 4 inches (22.9 x 10.2 x 10.2 cm)
Flameworked, sandblasted; borosilicate glass
PHOTO BY TOMMY ELDER

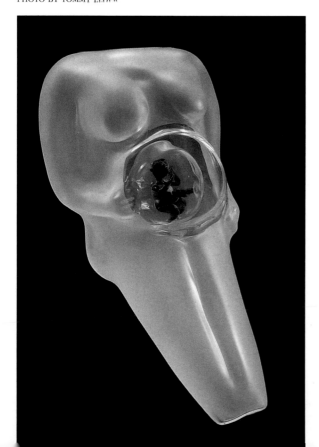

Washington; UrbanGlass in Brooklyn, New York; Public Glass in San Francisco; the University of Michigan; Niijima Glass Art Center in Niijima, Japan; Snow Farm in Williamsburg, Massachusetts; Worcester Center for Crafts in Worcester, Massachusetts; and Penland School of Crafts in Penland, North Carolina. She has also taught in Sweden, Italy, and Ireland.

Sally works both scientific and artistic glass. Her artwork is shown worldwide and has been featured in several books, including *25 Years of New Glass Review* by Tina Oldknow and The Corning Museum of Glass; Bandhu S. Dunham's *Formed of Fire: Selections in Contemporary Lampworked Glass*; *The Neon Engineers Notebook* by Morgan Crook and Jacob Fishman; *The Nature of Craft and the Penland Experience*, edited by Jean W. McLaughlin; *International Glass Art* by Richard Wilfred Yelle; and Lucartha Kohler's *Women Working in Glass*. Articles about Sally have appeared in *Glass Magazine, Glass Art, New Glass, Flow,* and *Vetro.* She has also presented papers on technical scientific glassblowing and written for numerous scientific journals. She has participated in many conferences for the Glass Art Society, the American Scientific Glassblowers Society, the Glass Music International Society, and the International Society of Glass Beadmakers.

With her background in both scientific glassblowing and artistic glass, Sally has found glass to be a limitless medium for expression and for showing flexibility, sound, sharpness, size, and movement. She says her desire is to continue working and learning her art for the rest of her days. Sally lives in Montague, Massachusetts.

Elizabeth Ryland Mears

What started for Elizabeth Ryland Mears as a response to glass's limitations in color turned into a surpassing gift: Her explorations of glass surface treatments have expanded her creative vocabulary and artistic vision. She engages viewers at the very edge of her intriguing pieces; what's on the surface is as important as what's beneath it. Using techniques as tools, rather than as ends in themselves, Liz creates much of her work to interpret the natural world and her place in it.

SHIFT: Bundle for Reaching Skyward, 2006
17 x 8 x 4 inches (43.2 x 20.3 x 10.2 cm)
Flameworked, sandblasted; borosilicate glass,
copper, waxed linen, steel
PHOTO BY PETE DUVALL

What Lies Beneath

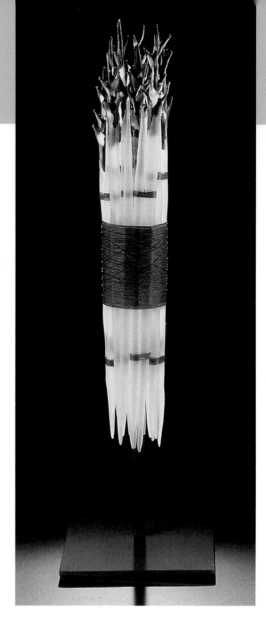

Bundle for Ice Time, 2002
21 x 5 x 6 inches (53.3 x 12.7 x 15.2 cm)
Flameworked, sandblasted; borosilicate
glass, luster, copper, waxed linen, steel
PHOTO BY TOMMY ELDER

From the time of my earliest memory, I have been a maker of objects. For me, the process of making objects has been an automatic response to living, akin to breathing. I follow a progression: formulating the concept for an object, designing the increments necessary to realize that object, and performing the hard work of fabrication until the object has life. Each step is part of a whole from which I cannot extricate myself easily or happily. The process is affirming for me; it is life-giving, in a way similar to the way in which eating and sleeping restore energy.

In the very traditional household in which I was raised, I tried to devise creative approaches to things that deviated from the norm. I often found myself totally absorbed in one project or another. On one occasion in grade school, my teacher gave the class an assignment to color a simple, mimeographed picture. I found myself absorbed in cutting out detailed shapes from construction paper and applying them, rather than performing the simple task she had assigned. I stayed after school and continued working for an hour or more while my teacher completed her own tasks. Only when my mother arrived with my two brothers in tow— and an attitude hovering somewhere between panic and fury—did I remember that I'd been instructed to come straight home after school that day.

My father was an engineer, so from an early age I was exposed to a linear, analytical way of thinking. Whenever we children had a problem to solve, we were taught to break it down into component parts, find the relationships, and synthesize the solution.

My father was also a builder of furniture. At one point, he added a wing onto the small house in which we lived. I helped with some of the handiwork, so I learned to use tools—and to love them. This project also helped me learn how to make parts and put them together in the correct sequence to construct a final object.

My father's father owned a hardware store. During my many childhood visits there, I learned to love bins of screws and bolts, washers and gaskets. The sights and smells of the place enchanted me. I love hardware stores to this day, I suppose because all those parts represent unlimited possibilities to me.

Both my parents gardened, as did all my grandparents. My grandparents' homes were surrounded by cutting gardens, hollyhocks, lilies of the valley, and flowering redbud and dogwood trees. These were magical places for a child with a curious, creative mind. Exploring them was a great adventure.

Elizabeth Ryland Mears

My father always had a vegetable garden somewhere in the backyard, and we enjoyed its fruits all summer and into the fall. My mother's gardening was different: She created wonderful panoramas of color. From an early age, I helped her dig in the earth and harvest the resulting blooms. A fresh bouquet almost always graced the house during growing season. Potted plants were brought in every winter to green the house. Tending them, too, became a ritual. Eventually I created my own indoor garden.

Now my gardens are filled with perennials. I look forward to that first blush of green as spring diminishes winter. I relish the view as some plants bloom before others have even begun to make an appearance, and during the cold months of winter I enjoy seeing the brown stalks of the past year's growing season. All of these cycles are part of my love of the earth and her fruits. That love has come full circle now: My daughter is a Master Gardener.

In school, in addition to making objects, I was interested in science. My parents' attitude was that although my ability to make objects from all sorts of materials was nice, my interest in science was much more legitimate. So, the latter was encouraged. Plant biology was fascinating to me. Learning how the cellular level of plants is organized and how cells cooperate with each other to move nutrients, water, and then synthesize starches—all of the macro and micro processes of plants were sheer beauty to me.

Still, as the time to attend college loomed near, I had no clear direction in terms of which of my interests to pursue. My mother encouraged me to become a botanical illustrator. I took a battery of tests, which showed that I had an extremely high aptitude in mechanical abilities. "Great," I thought. "What am I supposed to do with that?"

I took a pre-med course of study in college, so of course I had no time for art pursuits. Only now—looking back at all the activities in which I've been involved and those I've most enjoyed— do I realize that the battery of tests I took in high school was right on target. I have amazing three-dimensional visual abilities; I "see" things as completed pictures in my head. I have great mechanical gifts, and these gifts allow me to manipulate materials of all sorts adeptly.

Bundle of Twigs with Gold Leaf, 2001
9 x 19 x 6 inches (22.9 x 48.3 x 15.2 cm)
Flameworked, sandblasted; borosilicate glass, luster, brass, gold leaf, waxed linen, steel
PHOTO BY TOMMY ELDER

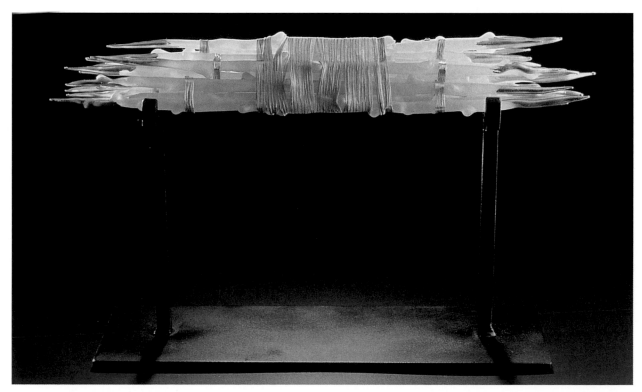

Elizabeth Ryland Mears

Shelter for Protection of Her Inner World, 2003
26 x 13 x 13 inches (66 x 33 x 33 cm)
Flameworked, sandblasted; borosilicate glass, luster,
horsehair, mica, quartz wool, copper, waxed linen
PHOTOS BY TOMMY ELDER

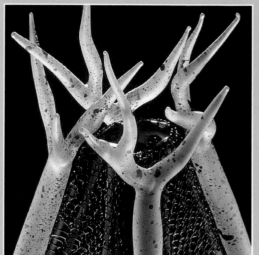

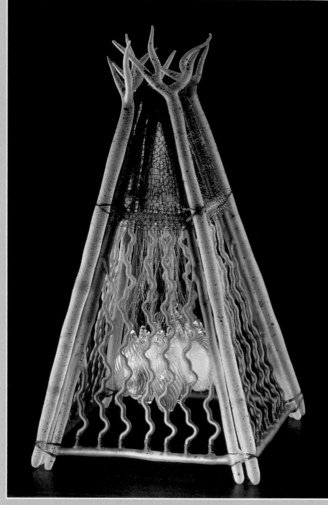

Shelter for Belief in Herself, 2004
22 x 13 x 10 inches (55.9 x 33 x 25.4 cm)
Flameworked, sandblasted; borosilicate glass,
horsehair, copper, waxed linen
PHOTO BY PETE DUVALL

Elizabeth Ryland Mears

FLAMEWORKING IS THE ANSWER

All my skills and history—my mechanical gifts, my exposure to nature, and my three-dimensional visual ability—came together at the focal point of flameworking. It was the answer for me. It was also, however, a late discovery. I was in my fifties. I'd raised two children and accompanied my husband around the United States and Europe during his career as a Navy pilot before I softened my first piece of glass in a flame.

The first time I entered a flamework studio was at Penland School of Crafts in Penland, North Carolina. My class wasn't scheduled to begin until the next day, but I went into the studio on my own for a look. The room was small, with its tables set up in a U-shaped formation. At each place sat a small torch. The room seemed cold and dark, and I wondered at the sparseness of it.

That first impression belied the activity that was to come. The next morning, the place came alive! The other students created a hum of voices that hovered in the room. We were shown how to operate the torches, and at once I began to manipulate glass softened in those animated flames. It was magic time for me! We busied ourselves, and the chatter quickly died away as each of us became mesmerized by the process.

As I began to work the glass, I thought to myself, "I love this. This is *it*! I will do this for the rest of my life, or for as long as I have the strength and ability." That first day happened in 1990, and my love of, and excitement about, creating objects at the torch has only grown.

In the 1990s, the world of flameworkers was relatively small. It was an exciting time of growth for flameworking, and I felt that a real sense of community existed. It was easy to get to know other artists who were considered to be the leading flameworkers in the country. Now, because of classes, seminars, and conferences at Penland and other craft and glass schools, the flameworking community has grown to include hundreds of excellent fellow makers. I am aided in my exploration of glass by the great creative energy and stimuli derived from both that first early contact with flameworking and the challenging work continually emerging from newer artists.

My Shelter for Endings that Beget Beginnings, 2000
23 x 14 x 14 inches (58.4 x 35.6 x 35.6 cm)
Flameworked, sandblasted; borosilicate glass, luster, horsehair, copper, waxed linen, wood
PHOTO BY PETE DUVALL

I am a proponent of the philosophy that when we are born, we come to Earth with a personality and a set of gifts, propensities, and abilities. If we pay attention to them, they lead us along a path to fulfillment. When those things we feel passionate about energize us, energy flows out and then returns to us, altered in some form by its journey. This energy creates a positive dynamic in all directions, reaching and influencing an ever-enlarging circle. Flameworking plugged me into just this kind of dynamic energy flow.

At Rest Beneath His Blanket of Leaves, 2005
8 x 24 x 12 inches (20.3 x 61 x 30.5 cm)
Flameworked, sandblasted; borosilicate glass,
luster, copper, waxed linen, steel
PHOTO BY PETE DUVALL

TECHNIQUES AS TOOLS

During that beginning time, when my connection
to glass was still new, the color palette of borosilicate, my preferred raw material, was very limited.
The colors that were available were not the clear,
bright hues with which I thought I wanted to work.
So, I followed the lead of other artists, such as
Ginny Ruffner, Susan Plum, and Janis Miltenberger,
by creating objects with clear glass. Later, once the
pieces were annealed and cooled to room temperature, I added color or other surface treatments to
my creations. Surface treatments permitted me to
go beyond the limits of the borosilicate palette.

Since then, boro glass colors have increased
greatly, but in my current glass creations I continue
to incorporate many of the early surface treatments
that I used to utilize. These surface treatments, in
addition to giving me a broad scope of color and
texture, help me work the glass and enhance its
surface in ways that best suit my creative intent.

I am fascinated by the quality of translucence,
which is found in few other materials but which is
afforded by glass. My creative bent is to stop the
eye of the observer at the surface of an object. I
like to create a surface for the eye to explore—a
skin that allows light to penetrate the material,
bounce around in the interior, and be emitted as a
translucent glow. Translucence imparts a very
different effect from transparency, which is adeptly
used by many artists for its magnifying and reflec-
tive qualities.

For most of my surface treatments, I begin with
sandblast etching. With this technique, I create
texture on the surface of the glass, lay down an
image, or simply make a wonderful matte surface
that can stand on its own or be manipulated
further. An etched surface appears soft, ethereal,
and mysterious, in contrast to the shiny, hard
surface of glass that has not been sandblasted. I
utilize both types of surfaces, along with many
other materials, in my mixed media and glass
sculpture.

I believe that artists, makers, and creators need a
broad range of techniques and materials from
which to draw in order to bring to fruition ideas

Elizabeth Ryland Mears

ONLY, 2008
11 x 10 x 8 inches (27.9 x 25.4 x 20.3 cm)
Flameworked, sandblasted; borosilicate glass,
luster, oil paint, waxed linen
PHOTO BY PETE DUVALL

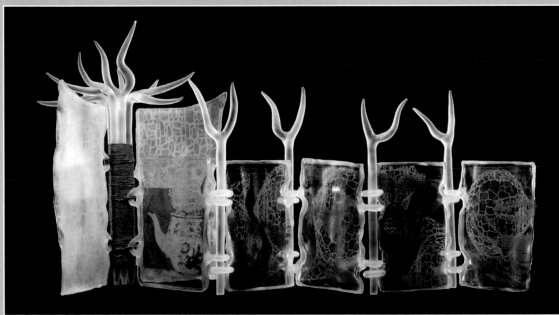

Teacup Conversation, 2008
13 x 20 x 10 inches
(33 x 50.8 x 25.4 cm)
Flameworked, sandblasted;
borosilicate glass, luster, oil
paint, waxed linen
PHOTO BY PETE DUVALL

New Journey, 2008
10 x 16 x 6 inches
(25.4 x 40.6 x 15.2 cm)
Flameworked, sandblasted;
borosilicate glass, luster,
oil paint
PHOTO BY PETE DUVALL

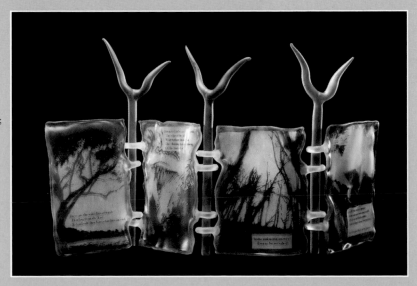

Elizabeth Ryland Mears

Bounty Conferred, 2006
8 x 12 x 12 inches
(20.3 x 30.5 x 30.5 cm)
Flameworked, sandblasted;
borosilicate glass, luster, sand,
steel, mixed media
PHOTO BY PETE DUVALL

conceived in moments of creative thought. I don't feel limited by "technique"; I use it to expand possibilities. Paints that are fired on or applied in the cold state, gold leaf used judiciously, and photographic images are but a few of the possibilities I explore.

I also feel artists need to utilize all the various techniques carefully. The techniques themselves should not be obvious in the pieces created. Rather, they should simply enable artists to complete their visions.

It is not unusual for students who have recently studied with a more advanced artist to incorporate newly learned techniques or to mimic their instructors. This is acceptable as part of the learning curve. However, at some juncture in their creative development, students who are no longer neophytes should aspire to develop their own visions and voices. Techniques are simply tools. Learn and master them, but use them only when the object you're making demands their use—in other words, when the use of a technique completes the piece rather than overburdens it.

The best times for me are when everything falls into sync. I am alone in my studio, totally absorbed in an idea and working on it, and time comes to a standstill. The materials and techniques being used in the process are not the primary considerations for me. The idea is the driving force.

Because I see things in my mind as clear images, I seldom draw detailed sketches. To tell the truth, I can't draw very well, anyway. Once the work has begun, the parts I have made dictate the parts that are to come. The glass speaks to me in its own special language. It tells me what it needs and leads me to achieve composition and balance intuitively. I feel great pleasure when I have the opportunity to revisit a piece, sometimes years later, and realize that I "got it"—that I created something substantial.

Hands On

Elizabeth Ryland Mears demonstrates how to apply to flameworked glass a useful array of surface treatments, including sandblasting, photoresists, lusters, metal leaf, electroformed copper, and oil paints.

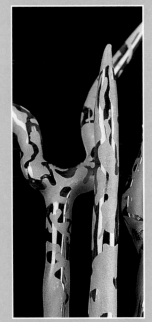

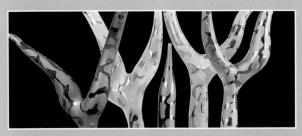

Today, color choices abound in glass used during the process of creating objects at the bench torch. You can make your own colored glass or use colored glass from a supplier. You can incorporate colored rods, frits, or powders in the interior of clear glass or on its surface. And as you make a glass object, you can mix colors in an array of combinations and layers.

Creating surface textures offers still other methods for adding color to the glass, extending your possibilities for artistic expression. These methods can be utilized after the flameworked glass object has been formed, annealed, and cooled. A primary method for adding surface texture is sandblasting. Although detailed directions for sandblasting are too lengthy to include here, I will discuss some methods of sandblasting that are used to create texture or images on glass and also methods for manipulating sandblasted surfaces. I recommend that artists make practice runs before incorporating these techniques on finished flameworked pieces.

1 In sandblasting, the surface of glass is blasted by a stream of compressed air containing grit. This process, which removes glass, can be used to simply etch the surface or, if it's done for a longer period of time, to carve into the glass. The entire surface can be sandblasted, or portions can be

Elizabeth Ryland Mears

protected from the eroding stream by an array of different masks. Specialized equipment is needed. For working with flameworked glass, I recommend using aluminum oxide as the grit and a pressure of 30 psi (206,843 Pa) or less for the compressed air stream. My sandblasting setup includes a lighted sandblast cabinet, a compressor, a vacuum system, a pressure pot for holding the grit (operated by a foot-pedal system), and a bucket of grit.

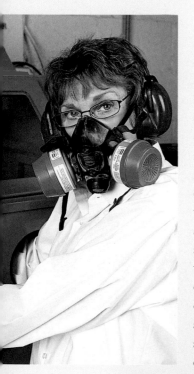

2 When sandblasting, I wear a respirator, protective studio clothing, and ear protection. Sandblasting causes glass dust to become airborne. Inhaling that dust can cause serious lung damage, so always wear a respirator. If you do not wish to invest in your own sandblasting equipment, check for a studio where you can rent time at a sandblaster. Your ears should also be protected, especially when you're near the compressor or vacuum system. A set of clothes to use at the blaster should be kept in your work area, so you don't carry glass dust into your living areas.

4 … and a photo of flameworked twigs that have received a light, even sandblasting, giving them warm, matte surfaces.

3 One method of sandblasting is to include no masking material at all so the glass is evenly blasted. This approach produces a smooth, matte finish, which can be manipulated further. Here's a photo of various colored-glass twigs that still have their shiny, flameworked surfaces …

5 Masking glass with white glue—applied with different tools and in varying thicknesses—can produce a variety of textures. Whatever method of application is used, the glue must be allowed to dry completely before any sandblasting is done. Sometimes I find it helpful to expose the opened container of glue to the air for a while, so the glue thickens before it's applied. If any glue remains on the glass once the blasting is finished, soak the glass in water until the glue softens, wash it off, and allow the glass to dry.

Glue can be applied with a brush, as in this photo. I'm laying the glue on in varied thicknesses. Using a stiff brush, such as a flux brush or a very stiff paintbrush, is helpful. You can even try an old

Elizabeth Ryland Mears

toothbrush. I sometimes trim the brush to augment the "raking" effect of the brush marks. Dragging a toothpick in the glue after it has set somewhat can further enhance the marks.

9 The glue acts as a barrier between the glass and the stream of grit in the sandblast cabinet. The random glue pattern that was applied is reflected in the unsandblasted areas on the blasted pieces.

6 The blasted glass shows the textural effect that brushed glue can provide.

7 A small applicator bottle with a metal tip, purchased at an arts and crafts store, is used to apply a pattern of white glue on the surface of a flameworked glass twig.

10 Using resist is another way to mask glass. Many different types of resist are available, including contact paper, masking tape, and resists made especially for sandblasting. Such resists are backed with adhesive; they must be applied to clean glass, and no air bubbles should be trapped underneath them. Each type of resist has a different tolerance to the pressure of grit and air, and some resists withstand the effects of sandblasting better than others. The resist I've applied to the glass here is soft and easy to cut to a pattern; however, it's able to hold up to a powerful stream of grit once it's been applied to the glass.

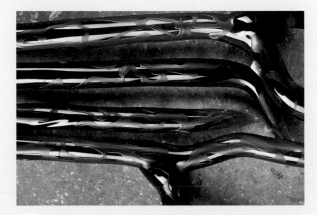

11 A design has been fully cut out after being applied to the glass. It is ready to be sandblasted.

8 The glue has dried, so these pieces are ready to sandblast.

12 After a design has been blasted, portions of the resist have been affected by contact with the stream of grit. To clean the resist, remove it from the glass and rinse it in clear water.

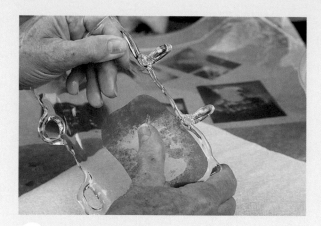

13 This sandblasted glass has been etched with a resist pattern.

15 A photoresist is applied to the glass and firmly smoothed. If air bubbles are trapped beneath the resist, I puncture them with a straight pin and then press down firmly in the area of the former bubble.

16 I'm removing the resist's clear, protective backing.

14 Photoresist is used to apply photographic images to glass. Several types of resist are available to which you can transfer an image by using a negative and exposure to ultraviolet light. The negatives are created most easily with a computer and sheet vellum or on a copy machine. The image used can be an actual photograph or some other image reduced to its black-and-white components.

In the photo, I'm using a sponge brush to apply adhesive to a glass surface. After applying the adhesive, I let it dry until it is clear and tacky.

17 The rest of the glass needs to be protected from the grit stream, unless it's supposed to be sandblasted. Blue painter's tape works well for this purpose. (Some different resists were photographed to illustrate different steps here.)

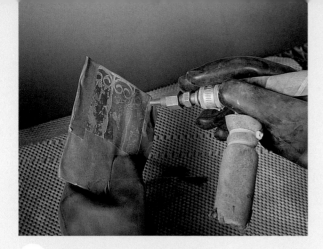

18 I hold the glass, with its photoresist, inside the sealed sandblast cabinet, and blast it with a stream of pressurized grit, which I control with a foot pedal.

19 The effects of sandblasting on a photoresist and tape are shown in this photo.

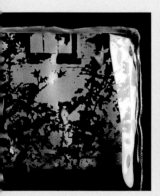

20 These two pieces of glass have had different photo images sandblasted onto them. Although the four methods of preparing a sandblasted surface that I've described yield different results, they all create a rough, "toothy," and absorbent sandblasted surface.

If this surface is left as is, it will have a somewhat chalky appearance. In this state, the surface can absorb dirt and oils. It can be sealed with a thin application of one of several different polymers, but you can also explore other possibilities—ones that take advantage of the tooth that sandblasting provides.

21 One treatment for blasted surfaces is to paint lusters onto them and then fire the pieces in a kiln. Here are some of the supplies I use for luster firings: several bottles of luster, a selection of sable brushes, brush cleaner, and rubber gloves. Also pictured are sandblasted twigs ready to be painted.

Lusters, which can be obtained from ceramic and glass paint distributors, are very toxic. Do not allow them to come in contact with your skin. When painting with them and when firing them in the kiln, a highly effective ventilation system must be used. I recommend leaving the studio when a luster firing is taking place, and leaving the ventilation fan running for several hours afterward before reentering.

22 I apply luster quickly with a sable brush.

Elizabeth Ryland Mears

23 The twigs are placed in the kiln for firing. My kiln is well ventilated, with a vented hood above it. The lusters are fired onto the glass at the annealing temperature of borosilicate glass—1050°F (566°C).

24 The luster applied to these twigs has imparted a glowing amber appearance to the surface of the glass.

25 Another treatment for a blasted glass surface is the application of metallic leaf. My supplies for a typical metal-leaf application include gold, silver, and copper leaf; a can of adhesive; various paintbrushes; and a soft cloth for burnishing. Gold, silver, and copper leaf, in various combinations and thicknesses, are available from art suppliers; you purchase a "book" that contains many sheets. Directions for applying the metal leaf are on the can of adhesive. Metal leaf is difficult to use at first and takes some practice, but it can be combined with glass to great effect.

26 The adhesive is applied to the sandblasted glass with a brush and allowed to dry until it feels tacky when touched with the back of a knuckle.

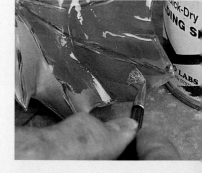

27 I pick up the gold leaf by placing a piece of waxed paper on top of it and rubbing the waxed paper with a finger. The static electricity created causes the sheet of gold leaf to cling to the waxed paper so that I can lift it up and apply it to the glass.

Elizabeth Ryland Mears

28 After applying the gold leaf, I burnish it with a soft cloth to ensure that all the gold has adhered to the surface of the glass. Any loose bits of metal leaf are removed.

29 Metal leaf can add great beauty to flameworked glass.

30 Applying electroformed copper to glass creates an interesting surface effect; however, specialized equipment is necessary. Artists can invest in a small electroform setup or find a studio that will rent one. The setup pictured includes a bath with electrodes, a copper strip, paint, brush, copper wire, and a jug of distilled water. In this photo, the glass rod is already suspended in the electroform bath.

In brief, the process goes like this: The glass is coated with a paint containing a suspension of metal, the paint is allowed to dry, and the glass is then suspended in a bath containing copper ions. A strip of copper is attached to the positive electrode, and the painted glass is attached to the negative one. An electric current is sent through the system.

Copper atoms migrate from the copper strip and are deposited on the charged paint on the glass. Over time, a layer of copper builds up on the glass. The current is turned off, and the glass is removed from the bath and cleaned.

31 Here, I'm painting the glass rod with the specialized paint containing a suspension of metal.

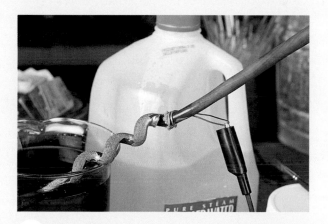

32 This twig has been suspended in the bath for several hours. Note the copper-deposit buildup.

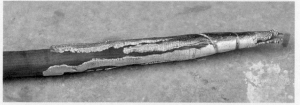

33 These photos show twigs that have received electroform treatment—one before and one after being polished with a brass wire wheel in a handheld rotary tool.

34 Oil paints can be rubbed into the surface of sandblasted glass. (In fact, if the glass is compatible with glass paints, the paint can then be fired on.) A typical setup for oil painting includes the paints themselves, cotton balls, cotton swabs, paper towels, and cardstock.

Oil paints adhere to the toothy surface of sandblasted glass in much the same way they adhere to canvas or board, and, based on my results, they seem to be as permanent on glass as they are on those surfaces. Here's the process: Oil paints are mixed to the desired color and then applied to glass with cotton balls and swabs or with the edge of a small piece of heavy cardstock. To make sure all the sandblasted glass is covered, it's important to rub the paint into the surface very well. Then, excess paint is wiped off. I use paper towels to do this, in much the same way as I wipe off a plate for printing.

37 When the desired density of paint is achieved, the glass is left alone for several days until the paint is cured.

35 Here, I'm using a cotton swab to rub in oil paint.

38 Of course, you can combine more than one of the techniques I've covered. Here, twigs made of colored glass have been sandblasted and then had copper foil applied to them.

36 Excess paint can be rubbed off with a folded paper towel.

39 These glass twigs have been sandblasted, coated with luster, and had silver leaf applied to them.

40 Glue was applied in random patterns on these flameworked twigs, which were then sandblasted and luster fired.

41 This glass was treated with brushed-on white glue and then sandblasted. It was then coated with two different firings of luster, and a coat of oil paint was added.

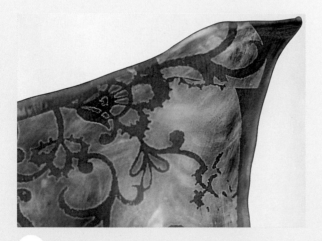

42 This glass received the works: a photoresist treatment, sandblasting, the application of a coat of luster, and, finally, oil paints.

About the Artist

Elizabeth Ryland Mears lives and works in northern Virginia, where her studio is surrounded by deciduous trees and gardens of her own fashioning. Immersed in this environment, Liz creates glass objects that interpret her relationship to both her inner and outer worlds, while using nature themes for that expression.

Liz has taught in many different venues, including Penland School of Crafts in Penland, North Carolina; Pittsburgh Glass Center in Pittsburgh, Pennsylvania; Washington Sculpture Center in Washington, D.C.; Touchstone Center for Crafts in Farmington, Pennsylvania; and Craft Alliance in St. Louis, Missouri. Her creations are held in private, corporate, and museum collections and represented in many leading galleries.

Liz is the author of *Flameworking: Creating Glass Beads, Sculptures & Functional Objects.* She serves on the board of trustees of the Creative Glass Center of America.

Solar/Lunar Family, 1996
30 x 13 x 6 inches
(76.2 x 33 x 15.2 cm)
Flameworked, sandblasted;
borosilicate glass, enamel
luster, brass
PHOTO BY TOMMY ELDER

Janis Miltenberger

When she decided to think big—literally and figuratively—in her captivating flamework, Janis Miltenberger started reaching her audience in an entirely different way. Her dramatic sculptures, including cages, are life sized; many of them reference mythological and biblical stories. Yet even while envisioning the big picture, Janis continues to work one piece, one series, and one step at a time.

Sealed Desire, 2007
33¾ x 19 x 5 inches
(85.7 x 48.3 x 12.7 cm)
Sandblasted, painted; borosilicate glass, oils,
colored pencils, luster
PHOTO BY LYNN THOMPSON

A Melting Pot of Souls

Looking back over my life as an artist, I can barely believe that I have spent my entire adulthood absorbing images, feelings, and thoughts and distilling them into objects. What an odd and wonderful way to communicate my view of the world to others! This gift of translation was my unexpected talent.

Use of the narrative has been around for eons; it was born with the first storytellers, actors, musicians, and poets who created stories from life's lessons and observations. Human beings intuitively understand these stories, metaphors, and parables. Even without conscious understanding, we still respond, because our bodies hold a deep memory of archetypal imagery.

I am not interested in assaulting my audience with the demands of this world. Instead, I try to reach inside and stir something much more tender. What interests me and drives my work is our common vocabulary. I interpret my work as an exploration—a way to reach out and connect with something intrinsic within us. My hope is that I connect with a part of my viewers that does not concern itself with conformity in our world, but seeks to identify and delight in our unique humanity.

There is a story I tell myself, a kind of creation myth: Our life expression comes from a melting pot of souls, which flows like an enormous river. The earth and every plant, mineral, and animal come from this source. Because all our roots sit in the same soil, we are more alike than we are different. Even DNA confirms this fact. Our commonality is what I seek to find and narrate in my work, which reflects a desire for my audience to experience the connections we share. I don't seek to exploit anything or give single, definitive answers; I hope to pose questions, draw new lines, and open doors.

CHILDHOOD

Growing up in Berkeley California, during the sixties and seventies, I experienced what I thought

Ally in Hope, 2007
34 x 15 x 10 inches (86.4 x 38.1 x 25.4 cm)
Sandblasted, painted; borosilicate glass, oils, colored pencils, luster
PHOTO BY LYNN THOMPSON

was a shared national reality, but which was instead a rare glimpse of something special. I was taught the Golden Rule, that it's what's inside that counts, and that we are all equal. Both my parents were liberal thinkers, even for that day and age. They were just left of the norm that I witnessed all around me. I now recognize this type of social atmosphere as being unique and beautiful, and I feel that it helped shape my vision of the world.

My childhood home was a huge, old, brown shingle house built in the early 1900s. I give a lot

Janis Miltenberger

of credit to this house. Its craftsmanship and its visual references helped shape what I value. I remember the knobs, the built-in cabinets, the small room under the stairs, and the feel of its wood under my hand. Most children are tactile and observe what surrounds them, but I now see myself as having been a very introspective child who was especially alert to detail. The house played in my imagination as a friend might. I considered it a separate entity, and I interacted with it while keeping its well-being in mind.

I also spent countless hours alone in my favorite backyard tree. Much of my time outdoors was spent observing birds and the colors and shapes of plants. My father worked as an urban gardener; I am sure he was nearby weeding, which he did endlessly, so I felt safe exploring.

One of the gardens my father tended was across the street from the home of Alexander Calder's sister. My father became acquainted with the woman, and he asked if he could bring me by to see some of the small sculptures in her home—sculptures Calder had made in his youth. By that time, I had been to museums and had seen some of the mobiles for which Calder received his acclaim. But I realized when I saw those early works in his sister's home that he had started as a young artist by creating small, intimate objects. He had been part of a family and over time had grown into this famous man. Somehow this connected the dots for me. Slowly, the idea of becoming an artist was forming.

Spring Psalm, 2007
35 x 10 x 9 inches (88.9 x 25.4 x 22.9 cm)
Sandblasted, painted; borosilicate glass, oils, colored pencils, luster
PHOTOS BY LYNN THOMPSON

My mother was in the process of getting her master's degree in biology at the University of California, Berkeley—I don't know, maybe I was five or six years old at the time—and she sometimes had to take me with her to deliver a paper or talk with a professor. I was lolling around in the halls of the old science building one day and came upon a permanent exhibit of exotic insects in one of the hallways. The exhibit both fascinated and horrified me. The natural world and all its creations were dramatic characters in my developing story.

Bird's Atonement, 2005
32 x 14 x 14 inches (81.3 x 35.6 x 35.6 cm)
Sandblasted, painted; borosilicate glass, oils, colored pencils, luster
PHOTOS BY LYNN THOMPSON

Fulfilled in Sight, 2007
29 x 9 x 9 inches (73.7 x 22.9 x 22.9 cm)
Sandblasted, painted; borosilicate glass, oils,
colored pencils, luster
PHOTO BY LYNN THOMPSON

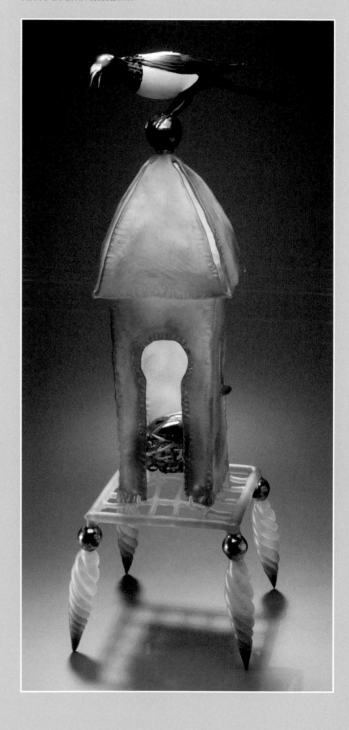

Both my parents valued creativity and supported my budding interest in art. I was dragged around to museums and concerts all the time. But as I got older, when I still wasn't thinking along the lines of a career that would bring in a steady income, well, their attitude was another story. But my parents' concerns made it all the better for me: I was rebellious and stubborn, and thus I determined that I would make my way in the art world somehow.

EDUCATION

In high school I spent all my extra time in the ceramics room. I wasn't the only student to find refuge in the social and creative outlet of clay: We had a group of regulars who virtually lived in that room. We went to our usual weekday classes, and then on weekends, we met for raku firings and, just for fun, attended lectures by well-known ceramic artists. I am thankful to have grown up at a time when the arts were valued and supported in public schools.

After high school I stumbled into a local community college that had a vibrant ceramics program. At that point in time, the San Francisco Bay Area was a hub for many dynamic ceramic artists: Peter Voulkos, Viola Frey, Robert Arneson, Ron Nagle, and my own instructor, Nancy Selvin. It was Nancy who introduced me to glass—albeit inadvertently.

Nancy had been friends with glass artist Richard Marquis for years, and their studios were in the same building. Dick was putting together a production studio. Nancy introduced me to him, and I spent the next three years working as one of his apprentices, blowing glass and doing various other studio tasks. Glassblowing offered the immediacy that clay did not—instant feedback on color and pieces that were out the next day, with none of the "waiting weeks" for results. I liked the atmosphere of working in a team and the choreography that makes up glassblowing. So, there it was for me: I kept it up and tried to gain the skills necessary to be a proficient glassblower.

A few years into my apprenticeship, I took two glass classes at the California College of Arts and Crafts in Oakland. Marvin Lipofsky, the head of the glass department, did his best to inform students about the larger community of glass artists. Artists from around the world came and shared their talents by demonstrating techniques unfamiliar to us. One of these artists was Italian glass maestro Gianni Toso.

Small Mercies, 2007
35 x 10 x 9 inches (88.9 x 25.4 x 22.9 cm)
Sandblasted, painted; borosilicate glass, oils, colored pencils, luster
PHOTO BY LYNN THOMPSON

Janis Miltenberger

Toso picked up a welding torch and gave us a simple lampworking demo, and my interest was sparked. Still, the use of soft glass and a welding torch would be the extent of my lampworking knowledge for a few years to come.

For the most part, art school was not my cup of tea. I didn't see the value in it. I seemed to be spending a lot of money developing a spin on what I was making. School was trying to wrap up my abilities into a market-ready product. The selling of myself left me dependent on the outside valuation of my talents. It seemed fake and, I hoped, unnecessary.

This is a cliché, but having been raised in the Bay Area, I had a strong need to just be me and not put on any affectations. If my work had to be specially packaged to sell, or I had to be made into a persona that did not reflect who I really was, then I wasn't sure that I wanted to be branded as an "artist."

THE WORK

Soon after that year in school, I moved north to Seattle, where I was introduced to some wonderful Pacific Northwest artists and began to feel that I might be able to find my way. I was working as a production glassblower and beginning to relax; I was only working with glass, without scouring over my outside image and worrying if I was an "artist" or even someone who made decent work.

For me, this was the trick: If I just worked and contained my thoughts within my own mind's eye, letting go of all competition and comparisons, then I made progress.

In the summer of 1991, I applied for and received a scholarship from Pilchuck Glass School in Stanwood, Washington. I enrolled in a lampworking class there with Susan Plum. It was wonderful. Susan was an entertaining, patient teacher. I had two uninterrupted weeks for the

With One Voice, 2006
17 x 21 x 4 inches (43.2 x 53.3 x 10.2 cm)
Sandblasted, painted; borosilicate glass, oils, colored pencils, luster
PHOTO BY LYNN THOMPSON

Janis Miltenberger

Articles of Faith, 2007
62 x 16 x 9 inches (157.5 x 40.6 x 22.9 cm)
Sandblasted, painted; borosilicate glass, oils, colored
pencils, luster
PHOTOS BY LYNN THOMPSON

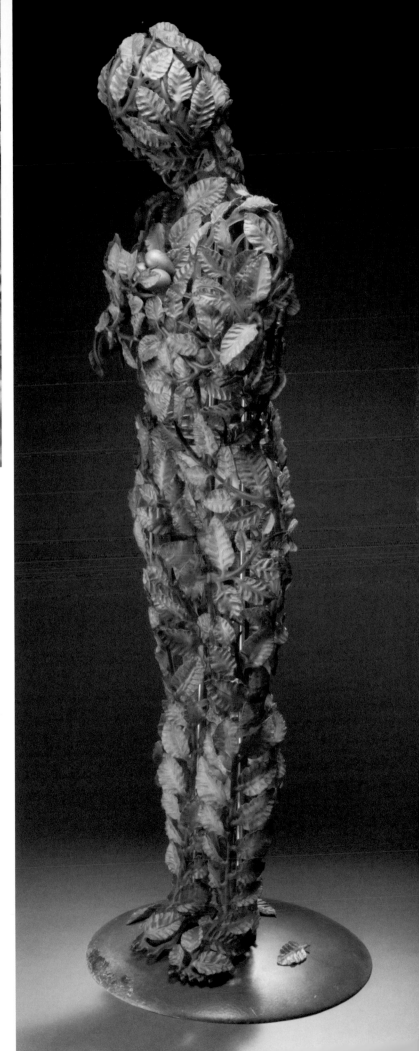

class, which was fantastic—at that point in time, I
had two small daughters at home. With all of my
prior glass experience, I took to lampworking
quickly.

Up until then I had held some unspoken
craftsman-type beliefs that governed what I could
and could not do with glass. For example, I re-
sisted using non-glass materials such as glue and
paint. Also, there remained a chasm in my thoughts
between my concept of what it means to be an
artist and the bottom-line economics of art. I felt
art should be attainable and not out of reach for
the average guy.

Recognizing these self-imposed rules allowed me
to make a decision: I would expand creatively and
develop a larger, more elaborate, and more
narrative range of work, while also catering to
customers by making smaller, more moderately
priced work. At this point, my work changed; it
became considerably more personal.

Initially, I created all of my lampworked pieces in clear glass. At this time, colored borosilicate was just coming onto the market. After working with the colors of soft glass, I found the borosilicate colors dull by comparison. This deficiency was beneficial to me in a backdoor kind of way: I was able to focus, as I hadn't before, on the story, texture, and intent of the piece, without being seduced by the gemlike quality of colored glass.

A common pitfall in lampworking is to make small, delicate pieces just because you can. I succumbed to this temptation. Without the constant urging of teachers such as Susan Plum and James Minson, I might still be doing that. Also, particularly if your work is going to be handled and shipped, you need to think through the function of your design and concentrate on good crafting. The last thing a patron wants is to break a precious piece of art accidentally and easily.

I recall my own teachers saying, "Work! Work in series, work a lot, and don't think too much." They were right, and this was excellent advice for me in particular. It is in the working that my story is revealed—not just to the audience, but to me as well. Working keeps me in the present. It keeps me focused. Often, the cumulative process of developing a series leads me to my next step. The work is a meditative practice that draws me to the next series.

For me, artistic progress is found in simple day-to-day efforts—in putting one foot in front of the other. I always harbor the small hope that my work will become more concise and illustrate my inner world with accuracy.

I practice intent. If you give in, at least somewhat, to your conscious intent, you move in the direction of your desires. I love the surprise of constructing a new piece and coming to the realization: "Of course I would make this piece. It is the embodiment of all my skills and work up to this point."

TEACHING

I really enjoy teaching. Sometimes the 12-hour days lampworking at Penland School of Crafts—fraught with burns and cracking glass—can be trying, but more often than not these intensive work experiences are invigorating highs.

When you teach, students in turn teach you a lot about what you do know and even more about what you don't know. Everyone's approach to the medium is unique. I think this is why I do not worry much about the replication of ideas. When someone copies another person's work, it is usually in order to work through a process of skill gaining. But never stay there too long—your voice and intent desire their own expression, and it is in them that you will find your gift to the world.

Having done both lampwork and furnace work, I find that each technique has its own advantages and best uses. As lampworking has grown in popularity, I have seen more work done off the torch that looks as if it were furnace blown. Some objects are best made at the end of a pipe and others on a torch. To limit yourself to one technique when you are also drawn to a different aesthetic is deadening.

In my experience, finding the technique that can uniquely enhance your expression is vital. Format is there for a reason. Each technique has its own stories and secrets. Expanding your abilities by employing different techniques only adds to your overall understanding of the substance.

Some of my approaches are very systematic, but I greatly enjoy crafting the work. The processes become second nature, and I enter this great zone where I intuitively know what to do and how to do it.

Students often ask me about the path traveled to "become" an artist. I still don't know if I have become one myself. I think most people never regard themselves as having arrived at such titles, so I recommend simply focusing on what is really important: listening, grace, and connection.

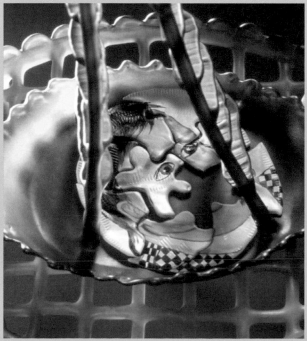

Made Whole, 2006
48 x 15 x 9 inches (121.9 x 38.1 x 22.9 cm)
Sandblasted, painted; borosilicate glass, oils, colored
pencils, luster
PHOTOS BY LYNN THOMPSON

Hands On

Janis Miltenberger demonstrates how to make a large glass sculpture that has multiple parts.

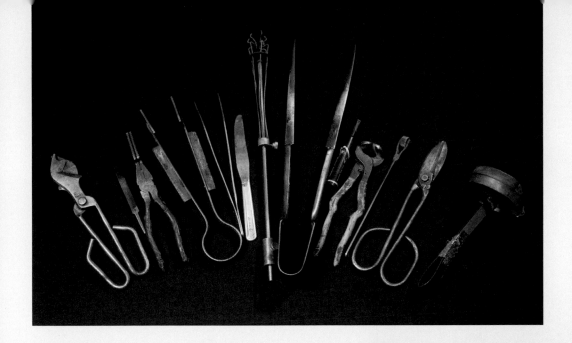

1 My tools, from left to right, are: diamond shears; a file; a texture tool (basically, a pair of pliers with a coarse file welded onto them); flatteners; tweezers; my favorite thin knife; big grabbers; jacks; a permanent marker; tile nippers; a texture roller tool; straight shears; and a funky squisher that I fabricated myself.

The only things not pictured are my graphite slab, glass rods, stainless-steel tabletop, National hand torch, and Herbert Arnold Zenit burner.

I want to say right off the bat that my work is annealed multiple times. Between just about every step shown in the how-to photos here, the piece I'm working is annealed. When in doubt, anneal! Consider the time you've already invested and how much more time it takes to repair cracks. When I get cracks, some are repaired easily, and others can't be repaired. The more I work, the more the glass teaches me about its needs and requirements.

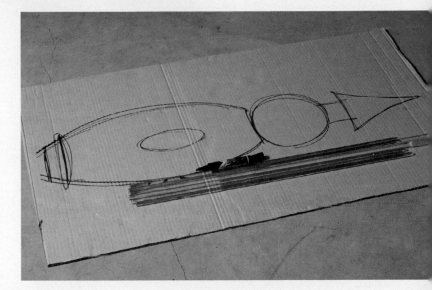

2 I always start with a generalized, full-scale sketch of the thing I want to make. The sketch serves two purposes. First, it helps ensure that what I'm making will fit into the annealing oven. Second, I use it as a pattern. I look at its proportions and think through how I'll go about constructing each element. The details figure in: Sometimes they are important to the construction, although more often they are complementary elements attached to the basic form.

Each area I've drawn represents a rod that I will have to bend to fit. This piece will be a cage. I pre-cut the rods I'll use for each area. Thicker rods are easier to bend than thinner ones, so I usually use ⅜- to ⁷⁄₁₆-inch (9 to 11 mm) rods.

Janis Miltenberger

5 All the rods must be attached to something to provide stability, so I make a series of rings that will divide the different sections of the cage. I'm bending a small ring here. This photo gives a good idea of what I mean by a broad, soft, hot flame.

3 I find that a broad, soft, hot flame works best for bending rods. To achieve consistent heating, I rotate the rod, as well as move it backward and forward in the flame. To one end I've attached a handle, which I'll remove before applying the rod to the cage. I always cut the rods a little long so I can hang on to one end.

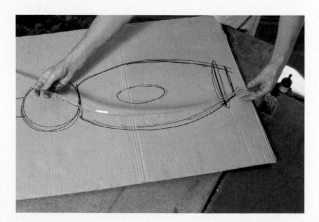

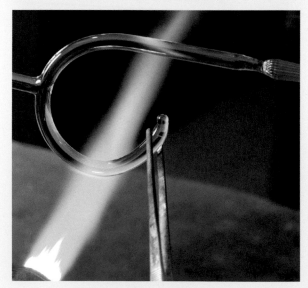

4 The sketch is my pattern. I don't actually touch the hot glass to it. If I'm working on a project that requires my touching the glass to the pattern, I draw the pattern on my stainless-steel tabletop.

6 I add a rod to the ring so I can hold it and control the form. I don't bend the rings to a pattern. I know the diameter I'm going for, based upon my drawing.

Janis Miltenberger

7 I use a graphite rod to smooth the seal. Getting the seal right—to look consistent at the join—is a trick. It takes practice. To work different areas of the ring, I often change the handle position by yanking the first handle off and attaching another in a different place.

8 I use my "squisher" paddle to help me shape the ring and keep it within one plane.

9 I start to assemble the rings and rungs by attaching two rungs to the two rings of the bottom section of my cage. Placing my level horizontally across a ring, I do the best I can, while remaining sane, to make the piece level and plumb.

One of the two rods acts as a brace; it holds the shape of the piece while I get the next join perfect. If I don't get the shape I want at this stage, I'm only making more work for myself later. The greater the number of rods added to the piece, the more daunting making any changes becomes.

10 I use a thick permanent marker to indicate where the rods will go. Doing so helps me lay the piece out well, without crowding my joins on the rings. When the rings are different sizes, as they are here, the rod-attachment layout on each ring is different.

11 Once the piece can stand on its own, I use a hand torch to fuse the rods to the framework. When I'm building a large or awkward piece, having a way for the piece to stand freely is a grand idea; it frees my arms for other tasks.

Janis Miltenberger

12 I usually add the rungs in opposition. Doing so keeps the stress even within the piece. If I were to add all the rods to one side before adding them to the opposite side, they would pull and distort the form, making it off-center. Alternating working on one side with working on the other keeps the piece even.

13 As I finish adding the fourth rung, I trim off some glass to make it fit.

14 These photos jump forward in time: I'm now adding the foliage and texture details. What happened between the last photo and these two? I added the rest of the rungs to the bottom cage section and also added a circular ring and several curved rungs to make the top cage section. I made all the leaves and annealed them; they sit at room temperature, ready to be attached. Now I'm using my hand torch to add the leaves and texture to the vertical rungs. I use the hand torch because a larger torch flame might hit areas that I don't want to heat, which could cause cracking.

15 I add texture to the rungs and stems with my texture roller. Most of the leaves, which are fragile, are attached in two places, which makes them more stable and helps them survive shipping and general handling. A second join also helps me work a leaf; the stability it provides prevents the leaf from slumping down as I work on it.

16 Now I create the base that the cage will sit on. The base is not fused to the cage; it is a separate element.

First, I make the ring and anneal it. Then I mark with a permanent marker where I want the rods to go. I will be giving the base what I call a "tennis-racket look"—a crosshatch of rods. I make the base in one sitting, keeping it all warm as I work. There will be a lot of stress in the glass, because there are so many attachments within a small area, so I find that thinner, 9/32-inch (7 mm) rods work best.

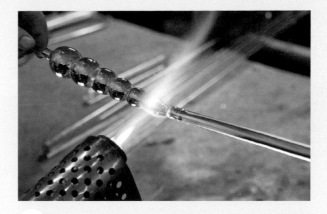

17 I really concentrate on the joins. They should be smooth, like branches growing from a tree. The viewer shouldn't be able to tell which part was made first; instead, the whole thing should flow together.

19 Here, I'm starting to build the legs that will support the base. First, I make a prototype leg and anneal it, so I can use it as a visual model; then I make the others legs to match it. A good plan is to use rods of the same length and thickness, so I measure out and pre-cut these rods.

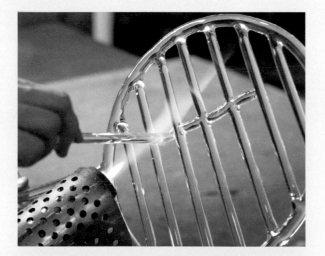

18 When I make the crossbars of the base, I straighten the lines with a knife.

20 I want to incorporate a cobalt-colored ball at the top of each leg. To make these balls, I apply cobalt borosilicate to the surface of a clear rod and then coat the cobalt with clear glass. Then I use diamond shears to define the ball shape. Once the shaping is completed, I make sure the cobalt ball is evenly heated, and then I keep the ball heated in an annealing oven kept at 1000°F (538°C) until I can apply the ball to the leg.

Janis Miltenberger

21 I apply a colored ball to each pre-made, annealed leg. The colored glass is applied hot to avoid cracking; colored glass tends to be temperamental.

22 Each leg, complete with colored ball, has now been annealed. I apply no more than two legs at a time to the base, and then anneal the whole thing. If you try to add too many elements at once to a piece that has this many joins and as much stress, it will just crack. I avoid the hassle by annealing in between attaching the legs. I still get some cracks, but not as many. I seal the cracks one at a time and anneal after each application of the torch to the glass.

23 I use both my bench burner and a hand torch to work the base. I also use a level on the base. It takes a lot of fussing to position the legs correctly; they should all be attached at similar angles to the base, and the base as a whole should remain level.

24 The very top of the cage will have a roof (or hat, of sorts). The roof is blown, so I pull points on heavy wall tubing that's about 2³⁄₁₆ inches (56 mm) in diameter.

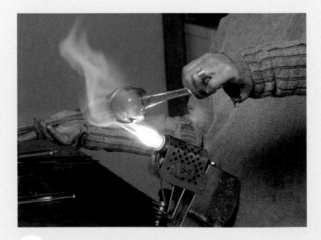

25 I wear (former) socks as arm protectors while I use a soft flame to achieve even heating of the tube.

26 I work the glass to get a cone shape.

27 I remove the closed end of the tubing, and continue to work on getting the shape right.

28 I've added a punty to what will become the top of the cone, and now I'm using my diamond shears to score a line where the open tube will be removed so that I can create a lip.

29 I've heated the lip and opened up this section of the cone. Now I'm using my jacks to expand the lip.

30 I'm still trying to get the shape right. The jacks sometimes double as a paddle that I use to help create a shape.

31 Much of the construction of the cage has now been completed. I've made three main areas of the cage design: the lower, larger body; the small sphere on top of it; and the blown section, which looks like a little, round house with holes, on top of that. While the cone is still hot, I size it to make sure that it will work with the overall form.

32 To create a framework to support the cone roof, I start by adding small bits of glass to the house section.

34 The cage and roof are now annealed, so they can be handled and examined for how well they fit together. These two elements will not be fused together; instead, the roof will sit on the framework I'm constructing.

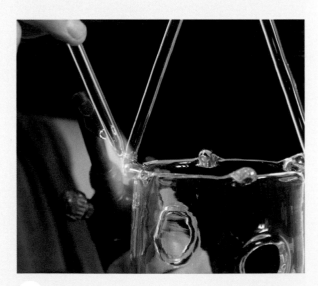

33 I add only two rods at a time to the framework, and then anneal before adding more. This is especially important when you are dealing with a room-temperature blown shape such as the house section. I'm careful with my flame; I don't want it to hit any other areas, or it could cause the house to crack. Also, I pay close attention to keeping the rods straight and correctly aligned.

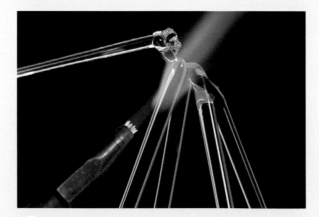

35 I've added two more rods to the framework, and have two more to go. Again, the whole piece is annealed before I add anything else. Once the main body of the sculpture is complete, there is more to be done, of course: I sandblast the surface, apply oil paints, and add an interior piece—a bird inside my cage. I've titled the piece *Encounter at Nightfall*.

For the past 23 years, Lopez Island has been Janis Miltenberger's home. The island—a small rock nestled into the northwest corner of Washington State—has a population of about 2,000. "We have a tight, supportive community," Janis says, "and although I hide away in my studio most of the time, my friends and community are there when I surface."

Janis says her husband, Bruce Botts, is "an incredible artist—of paints and prints—who qualifies as my better half. Together, we have constructed a commercial building that houses both of our studios, as well as some rental space. We enjoy creating spaces and doing so has helped even out our erratic income as married artists."

Their daughter Zoey is pursuing a career in law, and their other daughter, Ariana, is following a career in the visual arts and crafts. Janis calls her two children "the best of all my creations."

Janis has taught at Pratt Fine Arts Center in Seattle, Washington; Penland School of Crafts in Penland, North Carolina; Glasscraft in Golden, Colorado; and Mesa Art Center in Mesa, Arizona. Her work is featured at Thomas R. Riley Galleries in Cleveland, Ohio; CODA Gallery in Palm Desert, California, Park City, Utah, and New York City; Butters Gallery in Portland, Oregon; waterworks gallery in Friday Harbor, Washington; Pismo Fine Art Glass in Denver, Colorado; and Habatat Galleries in Boca Raton, Florida. Her website is www.janismiltenberger.com.

Love's Sacrament, 2006
36 x 10 x 10 inches (91.4 x 25.4 x 25.4 cm)
Sandblasted, painted; borosilicate glass, oils, colored pencils, luster
PHOTOS BY LYNN THOMPSON

LOREN STUMP
Cybil of Delphi Murrini Paperweight, 2007
Diameter: 4 inches (10.2 cm)
Lampworked murrini; vacuum encased soda-lime glass,
Schott crystal
PHOTO BY RICH IMAGES

LOREN STUMP
Vagiya, 1999
12 x 8 x 5 inches (30.5 x 20.3 x 12.7 cm)
Lampworked, sculpted, kiln assembled, murrini;
soda-lime glass, gold overlay, vacuum encasement
PHOTO BY RICH IMAGES

LOREN STUMP
Madonna of the Rocks, 2005
2¼ x 1½ x ⅛ inches
(5.7 x 3.8 x 0.3 cm)
Lampworked murrini,
cold-worked; soda-lime glass
PHOTO BY RICH IMAGES

KARI RUSSELL-POOL
*With All My Love—Sunflower
(Gardener's Valentine Series)*, 2007
16 x 16 x 2 inches (40.6 x 40.6 x 5.1 cm)
Flameworked, framed; flat glass, cherry wood
PHOTO BY ARTIST

LOREN STUMP
Prehistoric Crystal, 2007
7 x 6 x 5 inches (17.8 x 15.2 x 12.7 cm)
Lampworked murrini, kiln assembled, cold-worked;
vacuum encased soda-lime glass, Schott crystal
PHOTO BY RICH IMAGES

KARI RUSSELL-POOL
*Traditional Valentine
(Gardener's Valentine Series)*, 2007
16 x 16 x 2 inches (40.6 x 40.6 x 5.1 cm)
Flameworked, framed; flat glass, cherry wood
PHOTO BY ARTIST

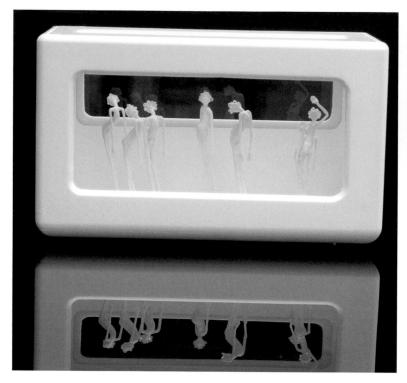

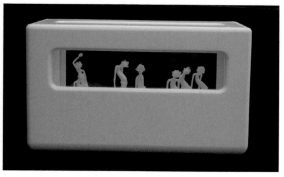

JILLIAN MOLETTIERE
Scene One: Take One, 2005
5 x 9 x 4 inches (12.7 x 22.9 x 10.2 cm)
Flameworked; soda-lime glass, plate glass, Corian
PHOTOS BY GATESON RECKO

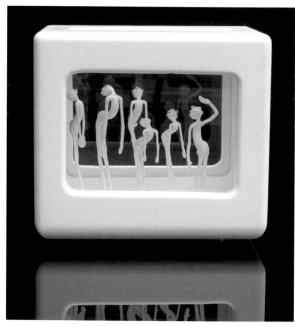

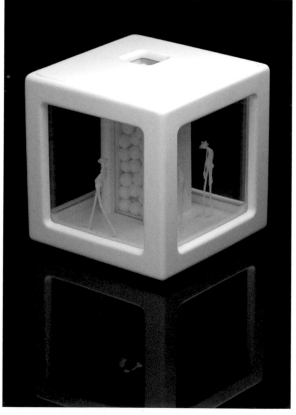

JILLIAN MOLETTIERE
Single White Cell 1.2, 2006
5 x 7 x 4 inches (12.7 x 17.8 x 10.2 cm)
Flameworked; soda-lime glass, plate glass, Corian
PHOTO BY GATESON RECKO

JILLIAN MOLETTIERE
Tower, 2006
8 x 8 x 8 inches (20.3 x 20.3 x 20.3 cm)
Flameworked; soda-lime glass, plate glass, Corian
PHOTO BY GATESON RECKO

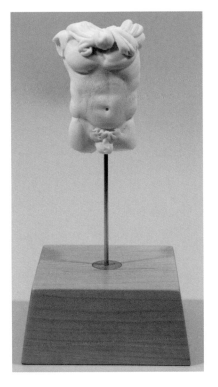

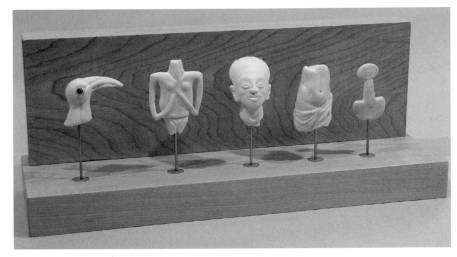

MARSHALL HYDE
Object Study 1.6.2004, 2004
6½ x 16 x 5 inches (16.5 x 40.6 x 12.7 cm)
Flameworked, acid etched; soda-lime glass, wood,
stainless steel
PHOTO BY ARTIST

MARSHALL HYDE
Object Study: Roman Torso, Man, 2004
7 x 3½ x 3½ inches (17.8 x 8.9 x 8.9 cm)
Flameworked, acid etched; soda-lime glass, wood,
stainless steel
PHOTO BY ARTIST

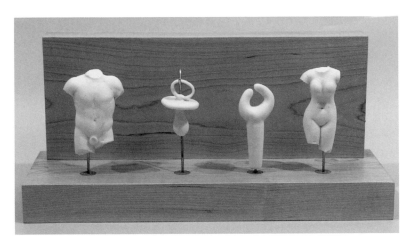

MARSHALL HYDE
Object Study 7.4.2004, 2004
6½ x 14 x 5 inches (16.5 x 35.6 x 12.7 cm)
Flameworked, acid etched; soda-lime glass,
wood, stainless steel
PHOTO BY ARTIST

MARSHALL HYDE
Object Study: Roman Torso, Woman, 2004
7½ x 3½ x 3½ inches (19.1 x 8.9 x 8.9 cm)
Flameworked, acid etched; soda-lime glass,
wood, stainless steel
PHOTO BY ARTIST

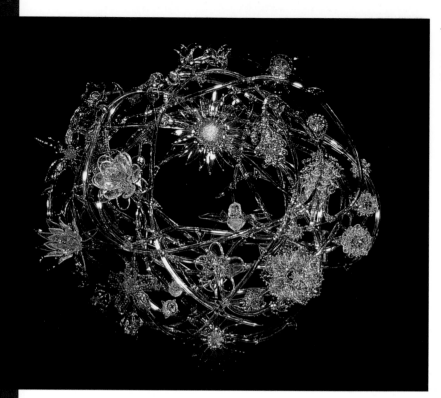

JAMES MINSON
Wreath, 2000
24 x 22 x 8 inches (61 x 55.9 x 20.3 cm)
Flameworked; glass
PHOTO BY ARTIST

JAMES MINSON
Octopus Chandelier, 2004
24 x 30 x 24 inches (61 x 76.2 x 61 cm)
Flameworked; glass
PHOTO BY ARTIST

JAMES MINSON
Jellyfish Chandelier, 2004
40 x 40 x 36 inches (101.6 x 101.6 x 91.4 cm)
Flameworked; glass
PHOTO BY ARTIST

JAMES MINSON
Thorned Chandelier, 2002
30 x 30 x 30 inches (76.2 x 76.2 x 76.2 cm)
Flameworked; glass
PHOTO BY ARTIST

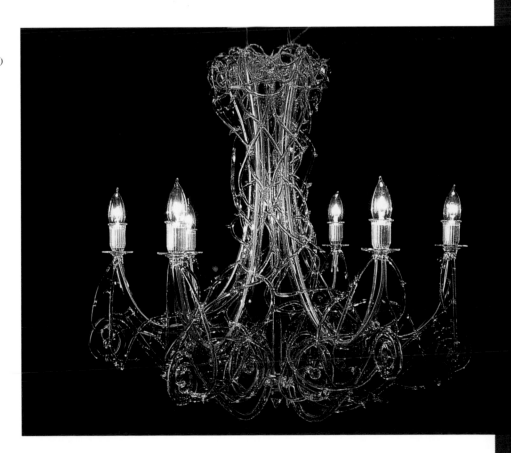

HANS GODO FRABEL
Hammer and Nails, 1977
9 x 12 x 6 inches (22.9 x 30.5 x 15.2 cm)
Flameworked; borosilicate glass
PHOTO BY ARTIST
COURTESY OF SMITHSONIAN INSTITUTION, WASHINGTON, D.C.

HANS GODO FRABEL
Large Cube with Imploded Glass Spheres, 2006
192 x 168 x 168 inches (4.9 x 4.3 x 4.3 meters)
Flameworked; borosilicate glass, mixed media
PHOTO BY ARTIST

HELENA KÅGEBRAND
*And the Phantom Said: I Know What to Look
for in You*, 2005
11¹³⁄₁₆ x 7⅞ x 3⅛ inches (30 x 20 x 8 cm)
Flameworked; borosilicate glass, black oxides
PHOTO BY RICHARD WILLENBRANDS

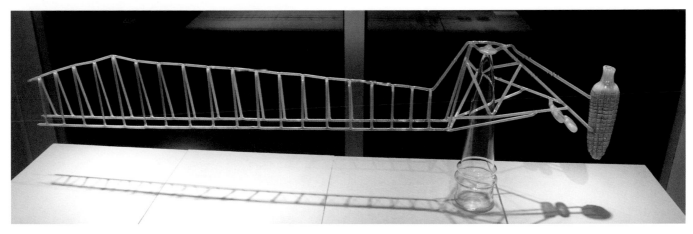

CHRISTOPHER MCELROY
Weight of the Maize, 2006
11½ x 41 x 8 inches (29.2 x 104.1 x 20.3 cm)
Flameworked; borosilicate glass
PHOTO BY ADAM GRABER
COURTESY OF DEL VIDRIO GALLERY

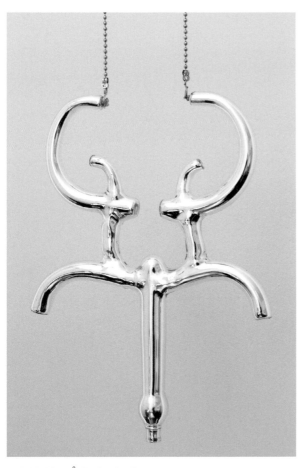

CHRISTOPHER MCELROY
Word to Print I, 2006
4 x 6 x 3½ inches (10.2 x 15.2 x 8.9 cm)
Flameworked, cold-worked; borosilicate glass
PHOTO BY ADAM GRABER
COURTESY OF DEL VIDRIO GALLERY

HELENA KÅGEBRAND
Silverme, 2007
15¾ x 7⅞ x 1³⁄₁₆ inches (40 x 20 x 3 cm)
Flameworked, silver plated; borosilicate glass
PHOTO BY TORD LUND

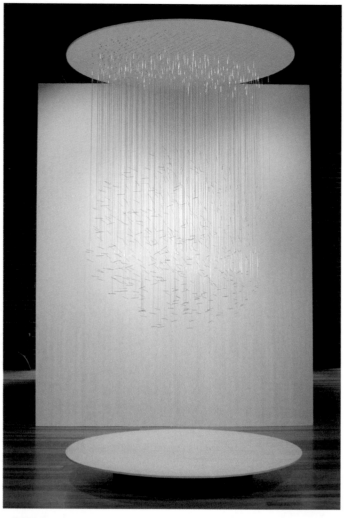

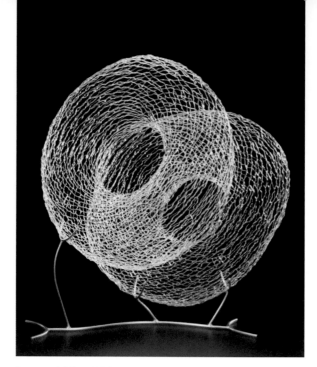

BENNETT BATTAILE
Tube Wave, 2004
16 x 15 x 7 inches (40.6 x 38.1 x 17.8 cm)
Flameworked; glass, stainless steel
PHOTO BY BILL BACHHUBER

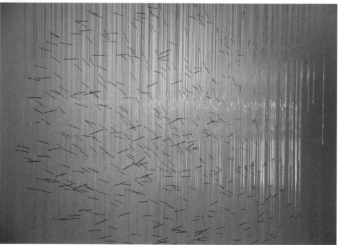

BENNETT BATTAILE
Breeze, 2005
108 x 60 x 60 inches (2.7 x 1.5 x 1.5 m)
Flameworked, machined; glass, plywood
PHOTOS BY BILL BACHHUBER

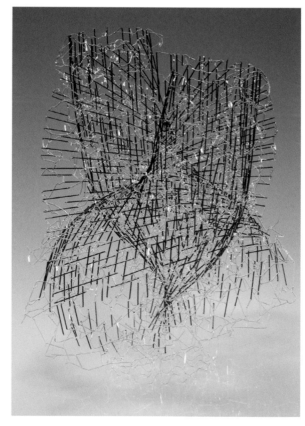

BENNETT BATTAILE
Deja Vu, 2003
13 x 13 x 13 inches (33 x 33 x 33 cm)
Flameworked; glass
PHOTO BY BILL BACHHUBER

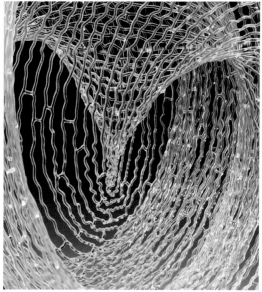

BENNETT BATTAILE
Mirage For Susan, 2006
12 x 13 x 6 inches (30.5 x 33 x 15.2 cm)
Flameworked; glass
PHOTOS BY BILL BACHHUBER

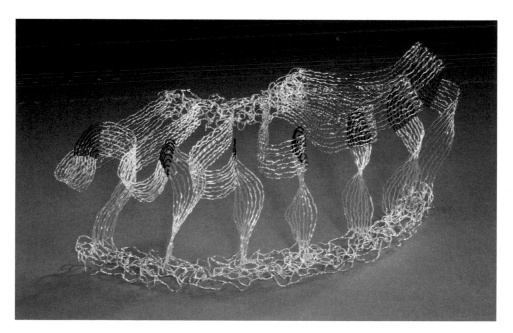

BENNETT BATTAILE
Key Frame, 2006
8 x 17 x 9 inches (20.3 x 43.2 x 22.9 cm)
Flameworked; glass
PHOTO BY BILL BACHHUBER

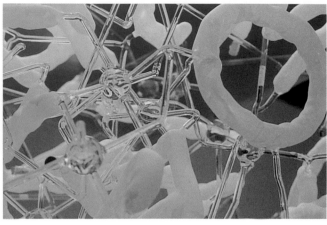

JILL REYNOLDS
Molecula, 2003
Flameworked, blown, fused; borosilicate glass, acrylic
paint, corks, ultra-violet light
PHOTOS BY ARTIST

JILL REYNOLDS
Revision, 2005
14 x 12 inches (35.6 x 30.5 cm)
Flameworked, blown, fused; borosilicate glass, brick,
monofilament, soda-lime vessel, water
PHOTOS BY DANIEL SPITZER
MADE FOR THE BEACON INSTITUTE FOR RIVERS AND ESTUARIES

JILL REYNOLDS
Matter, 2003
72 x 40 x 16 inches (182.9 x 101.6 x 40.6 cm)
Flameworked, blown, heat shaped; borosilicate tubing, electric pump, blue water
PHOTO BY ARTIST

JILL REYNOLDS
Table of Elements, 2003
4 x 5 x 5 feet (1.2 x 1.5 x 1.5 m)
Flameworked, found, altered; borosilicate glass and labware, other mixed materials, plate glass, plywood box
PHOTOS BY MUSEUM OF GLASS

163

JUDITH PFAFF
Fuchi No Iro, 1992
96 x 60 x 31 inches (2.4 x 1.5 x 0.8 m)
Wire, wool, steel, tin, glass
PHOTO BY ARTIST

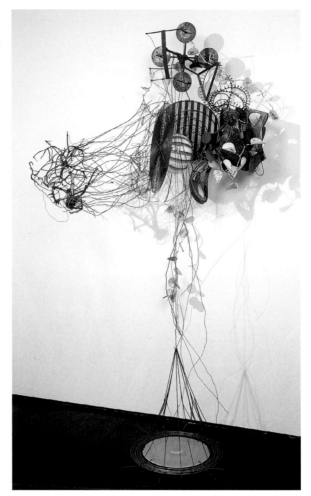

JUDITH PFAFF
Moxibustion, 1994
35 x 20 x 14 feet (10.7 x 6.1 x 4.3 m)
Heat and gravity shaped; glass, fiberglass,
steel, tar, plant material
PHOTO BY ARTIST

BANDHU SCOTT DUNHAM
Steam Engine #3, 2002
36 x 30 x 15 inches (91.4 x 76.2 x 38.1 cm)
Lampworked; borosilicate glass, luster
PHOTO BY CHRISTOPHER MARCHETTI
COLLECTION OF LAURA HOWAT

BANDHU SCOTT DUNHAM
Valkor "B" Series Marble Run, 2007
26 x 20 x 10 inches (66 x 50.8 x 25.4 cm)
Lampworked; borosilicate glass
PHOTO BY ARTIST

FREDERICK BIRKHILL
Infinity Bottle, 2006
12 x 5½ x 7 inches (30.5 x 14 x 17.8 cm)
Flameworked, blown, glass montage technique;
soda-lime glass, wood box with mirrors
PHOTOS BY ARTIST

FREDERICK BIRKHILL
Nested Montage Bowl, 2006
2½ x 5 x 5 inches (6.4 x 12.7 x 12.7 cm)
Flameworked, blown, glass montage technique; soda-lime glass
PHOTO BY ARTIST

FREDERICK BIRKHILL
Quilt Vessel, 2006
6 x 2½ x 2½ inches (15.2 x 6.4 x 6.4 cm)
Flameworked, blown; sheet glass, soda-lime glass
PHOTO BY ARTIST

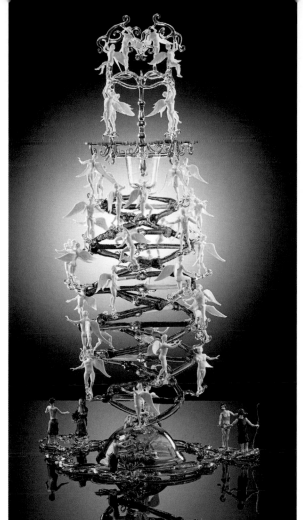

LUCIO BUBACCO
D.N.A., 2006
70 x 15 x 20 inches (177.8 x 38.1 x 50.8 cm)
Flameworked, blown; soft glass
PHOTOS BY STUDIO NORBERT HEYL

LUCIO BUBACCO
Birth of a Cerebral Flame, 2007
44 x 20 x 20 inches (111.8 x 50.8 x 50.8 cm)
Flameworked, blown; soft glass, gold leaf
PHOTOS BY STUDIO NORBERT HEYL

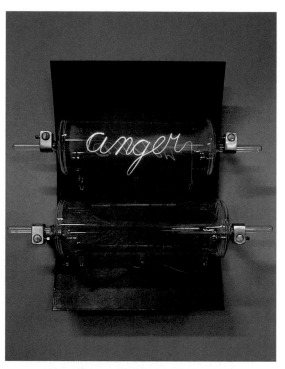

WAYNE STRATTMAN
Art and Disability, 2000
18 x 18 x 5 inches (45.7 x 45.7 x 12.7 cm)
Lathed, flameworked; borosilicate glass, nichrome wire,
tungsten, metal seals, inert gas, low voltage power supply
PHOTOS BY CHELYNN TETREAULT

WAYNE STRATTMAN
Rocket, 2007
26 x 5½ x 5½ inches (66 x 14 x 14 cm)
Lathed, flameworked, water jet cut, silvered, filled;
borosilicate glass, plasma gas mixture, high voltage
power supply
PHOTO BY ERIC STAROSIELSKI

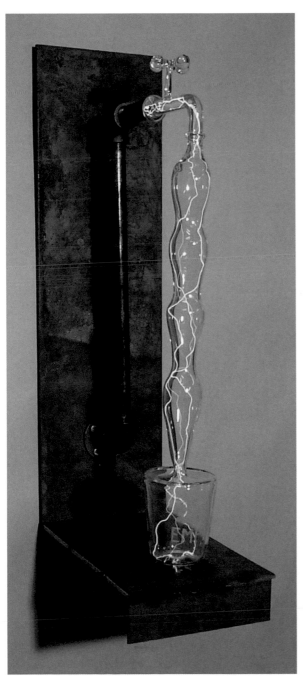

WAYNE STRATTMAN
Still Empty, 2002
31 x 13½ x 8 inches (78.7 x 34.3 x 20.3 cm)
Welded, flameworked; steel, borosilicate glass,
inert gas, power supply
PHOTO BY CHELYNN TETREAULT

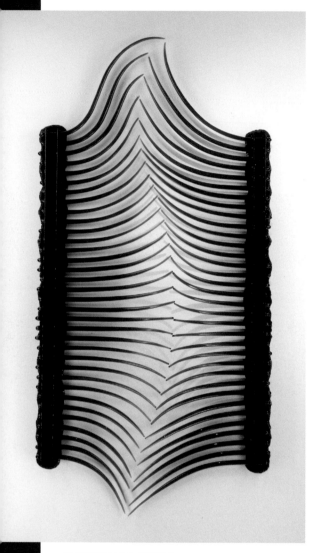

ROBERT MICKELSEN
American Icons, 2007
22 x 10 x 10 inches
(55.9 x 25.4 x 25.4 cm)
Flameworked, sculpted, blown,
graal technique; glass
PHOTO BY DAN ABBOTT

ROBERT MICKELSEN
Rising Wave, 2007
76 x 35 x 10 inches (193 x 88.9 x 25.4 cm)
Flameworked; glass, steel, rubber
PHOTO BY DAN ABBOTT

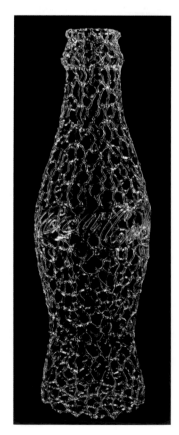

ROBERT MICKELSEN
Coca-Cola, 2007
30 x 9 x 9 inches (76.2 x 22.9 x 22.9 cm)
Flameworked; glass
PHOTO BY DAN ABBOTT

ROBERT MICKELSEN
Taming a Blue Giraffe, 2006
35 x 14 x 8 inches (88.9 x 35.6 x 20.3 cm)
Flameworked, sculpted, blown, resist sandblasted,
electroformed; glass, steel, copper, patina
PHOTOS BY DAN ABBOTT

AMY JOHNSON
Tubes of You (White) Necklace, 2005
22 x 1¹⁵/₁₆ x 1¹⁵/₁₆ inches (55.9 x 4.9 x 4.9 cm)
Flameworked, heat and gravity shaped, poked, signed
with handmade murrini; dots, soda-lime glass
PHOTO BY ARTIST

AMY JOHNSON
Tubes of You (Blue) Necklace, 2005
22 x 1¹⁵/₁₆ x 1¹⁵/₁₆ inches (55.9 x 4.9 x 4.9 cm)
Flameworked, heat and gravity shaped, poked, signed
with handmade murrini; dots, soda-lime glass
PHOTO BY ARTIST

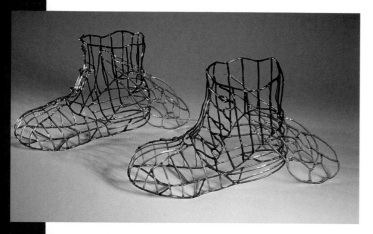

TINA BETZ
Baby Steps, 2000
3½ x 6 x 2 inches (8.9 x 15.2 x 5 cm)
Flameworked; soda-lime glass
PHOTO BY BRANTLEY CARROLL

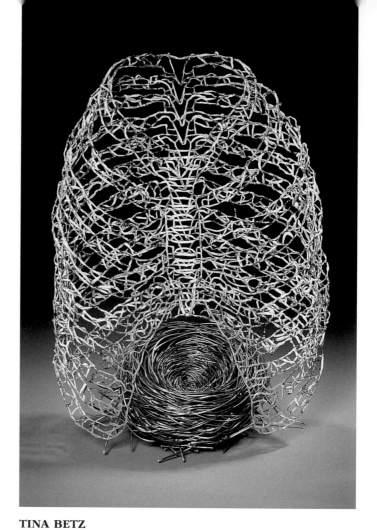

TINA BETZ
Body Baskets (Home Is Where the Heart Is), 2000
16 x 11 x 5 inches (40.6 x 27.9 x 12.7 cm)
Flameworked; enamel, soda-lime glass
PHOTO BY BRANTLEY CARROLL

HUBERT KOCH
Untitled, 1996
5⅛ inches (13 cm) high
Flameworked, montage technique; rods of enamel glass
PHOTO BY EBERHARDT RENNO

HUBERT KOCH
Untitled, 1993
6¹¹⁄₁₆ inches (17 cm) high
Flameworked, montage technique; rods of enamel glass
PHOTO BY EBERHARDT RENNO

GIANNI TOSO
Gianni Visits Marvin; CCAC, 1976, 1989
7 x 18 x 15 inches (17.8 x 45.7 x 38.1 cm)
Kiln-fused, flameworked; Venetian soda-lime glass
PHOTO BY KAPLAN MODERN GALLERY

GIANNI TOSO
View from Mulberry Street (NY), 1992
30 x 17 x 11½ inches (76.2 x 43.2 x 29.2 cm)
Kiln-fused, flameworked; Venetian soda-lime glass
PHOTO BY ARTIST

DONI HATZ
Floral Chalice, 1995
10 x 5 x 5 inches (25.4 x 12.7 x 12.7 cm)
Flameworked, heat and gravity shaped, fused;
borosilicate glass
PHOTO BY SCOTT WALKER

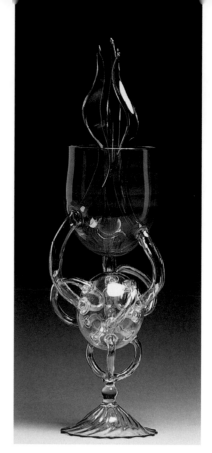

DONI HATZ
Goblet of Fire, 2003
18 x 7 x 7 inches (45.7 x 17.8 x 17.8 cm)
Flameworked, heat and gravity shaped;
ruby and amber colored glass tubes,
borosilicate glass tubing, gold, platinum
PHOTO BY MARK CHEADLE

DONI HATZ
Medusa, 1999
15 x 15 x 12 inches (38.1 x 38.1 x 30.5 cm)
Flameworked, heat and gravity shaped; glass
2-liter flask, borosilicate glass tubing, neon
PHOTO BY ARTIST

DONI HATZ
Nesting Robin's Egg, 2006
8 x 6 x 6 inches (20.3 x 15.2 x 15.2 cm)
Flameworked, heat and gravity shaped; glass tubing
PHOTO BY MARK CHEADLE

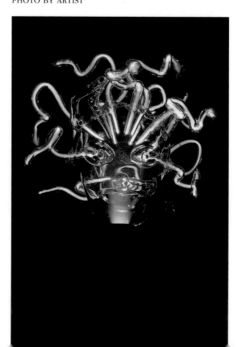

BRIAN KERKVLIET
Inspirational Narrative, Oil Lamp Menorah, 2002
20 x 12 x 8 inches (50.8 x 30.5 x 20.3 cm)
Flameworked, blown, sculpted, hot appliqué,
fused, foiled, soldered; copper, soda-lime and
borosilicate glasses
PHOTO BY ARTIST

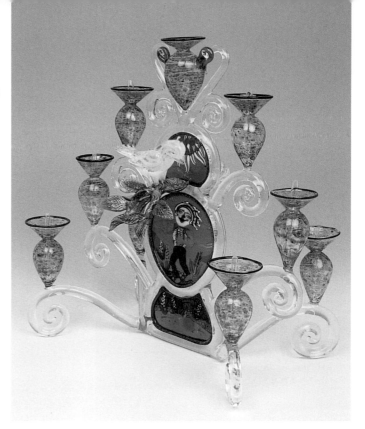

RICK AYOTTE
Yellow Waterlily, 2001
3½ x 5½ x 5½ inches (8.9 x 14 x 14 cm)
Flameworked, encased; soda-lime glass
PHOTO BY MELISSA AYOTTE

RICK AYOTTE
Mountain Bluebirds, 1992
3 x 3½ x 3½ inches (7.6 x 8.9 x 8.9 cm)
Flameworked, encased; soda-lime glass
PHOTO BY MELISSA AYOTTE

JDC ROMAN
Koi Fish, 2007
16 x 12 inches (40.6 x 30.5 cm)
Flameworked, blown, cold-worked, marvered, sand carved, sandblasted; hollow and solid borosilicate glass
PHOTOS BY ARTIST

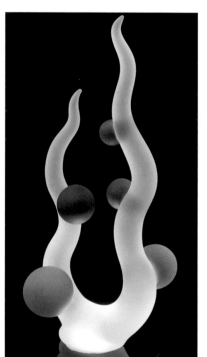

JDC ROMAN
Wave of Spheres, 2006
10 x 5 x 5 inches (25.4 x 12.7 x 12.7 cm)
Flameworked, cold-worked, marvered, sandblasted; borosilicate and colorsilicate glass
PHOTO BY ARTIST

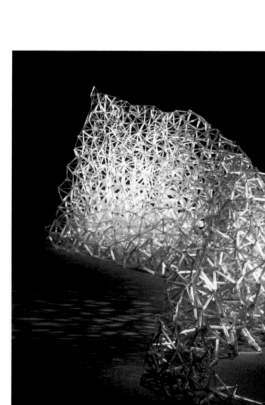

HARUMI YUKUTAKE
Untitled, 1999
82 11/16 x 354 5/16 x 137 3/4 inches (2.1 x 9 x 3.5 m)
Hand blown; glass tubes, stainless cable and fastener
PHOTO BY ARTIST

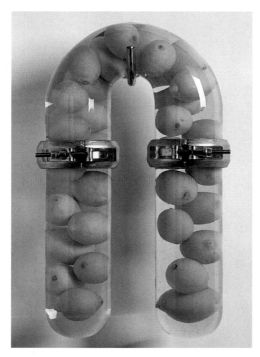

DONALD LIPSKI
Water Lilies #36, 1990
36 x 18 x 5 inches (91.4 x 45.7 x 12.7 cm)
Flameworked; acid wasteline tubing, stainless
steel, lemons, preservative solution
PHOTO BY DOROTHY ZEIDMAN
COLLECTION OF PABLO PALAZUELO, BARCELONA, SPAIN

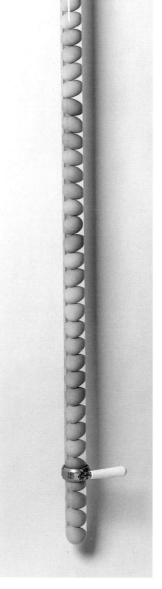

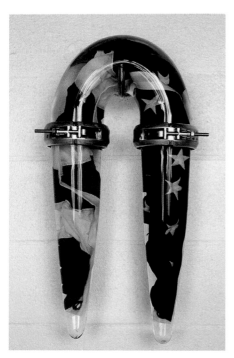

DONALD LIPSKI
Poxabogue Pond No. 31, 1995
27 x 14 x 6 inches (68.6 x 35.6 x 15.2 cm)
Acid wasteline tubing, flag, preservative solu-
tion, stainless steel
PHOTO BY ARTIST

DONALD LIPSKI
Poxabogue Pond No. 27, 1995
82 x 13 x 3 inches (208.3 x 33 x 7.6 cm)
Flameworked; acid wasteline tubing with hot glass by
Michael Scheiner, stainless steel, Teflon, eggs, preservative
solution
PHOTOS BY DOROTHY ZEIDMAN
COLLECTION OF TERRI HYLAND

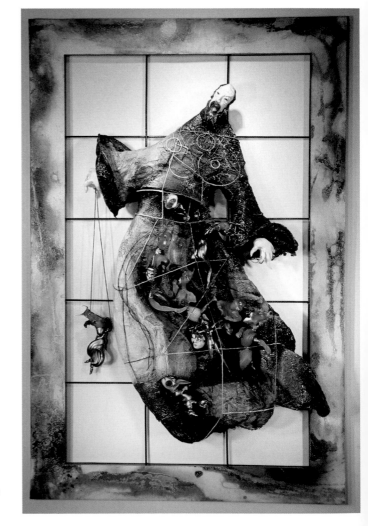

PAT OWENS
Storm at Galilee, 2007
24 x 19 x 11½ inches (61 x 48.3 x 29.2 cm)
Flameworked, electroformed, mounted, lacquered,
printed; patina, copper, steel, copper wire, cloth,
bronze wire screen, soda-lime glass
PHOTO BY ARTIST

PAT OWENS
Temptation of Anthony, 2007
35 x 23 x 4 inches (88.9 x 58.4 x 10.2 cm)
Flameworked, electroformed, lacquered,
mounted, painted, welded; patina, copper,
wire cloth, steel wire, wood, soda-lime glass
PHOTO BY ARTIST

PAT OWENS
Rebecca at the Well, 2007
18⅜ x 30½ x 4½ inches
(46.7 x 77.5 x 11.4 cm)
Flameworked, electroformed,
mounted, lacquered, painted;
patina, copper, steel wire frame,
cloth, bronze wire screen,
soda-lime glass
PHOTO BY ARTIST

PAT OWENS
A Cynic's Quartet: Politicians, Pop Culture, CEO, The Body Politic, 2006
Each: 8 x 8 x 2½ inches (20.3 x 20.3 x 6.4 cm)
Flameworked, electroformed; enamel, patina, copper, plate glass, soda-lime glass
PHOTO BY ARTIST

Ingalena Klenell

The essences of the natural Swedish landscape and its seasonal transformations are given graceful and free expression in the glasswork of Ingalena Klenell. Her large-scale pieces are designed to play with light and transparency as they communicate with nature—and about the human relationship to it. Flameworking and kiln forming both assume important, and very different, roles in Ingalena's artistic expression.

Dry Flowers, 2006
Diameter: 39 inches (99.1 cm) each
Kiln formed; float glass
PHOTO BY RAGNAR KLENELL

Chaos and Order, Fluent and Solid

My home and my studio in western Sweden are situated close to a lake. The view outside my window is a never-ending story, as the water communicates with the sun and the wind. Even if the deep lake is late in warming up, it's still a wonderful lake for swimming. And in winter, when everything is white and brittle, I love to skate on the ice.

Summertime, when a green curtain of birch leaves hides the tempting blue, is a powerful source of inspiration for me, with all its scenes capturing the diversity of nature. The shift from open water to silent winter surface—the exact moment when it goes from fluent to solid—is magic. After the lake freezes, everything is silent and calm. Chaos shifts into form.

I wait intensely for this time every year.

Nature finds the moment when everything is ready for a change. Water becomes ice, which lasts for several months. January is clear, the air is transparent, and it's a good time to work with glass.

I sometimes work a lot with recycled glass and glass of uncertain provenance, so I have done a lot of investigating into the nature of the glass I've found. In a way, it's like getting to know a new personality. Curiosity about that new personality carries me through various experiments. The most important information is the point at which the glass goes from fluent to a material full of tensions.

Sometimes I think a particular piece of glass is a special kind that can show or do something new. That is tremendously exciting for me, because I think of glasswork as a way to explore and investigate limits—the limits of both techniques and myself—and to transcend them.

The French philosopher Simone Weil's argument that vulnerability is the sign of existence is something that has touched me deeply and inspired me since the beginning of my life as an artist. I find this belief connected to glass, both as a material and as a medium with possibilities. The vulnerabili-

Cathedral, 2003
175 x 110 inches (444.5 x 279.4 cm)
Kiln formed, crocheted; float glass
PHOTOS BY LARS JAKOBSSON

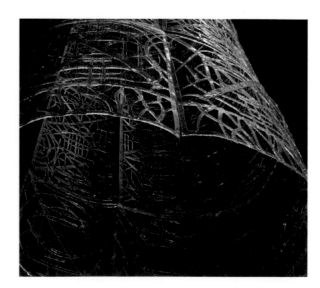

Ingalena Klenell

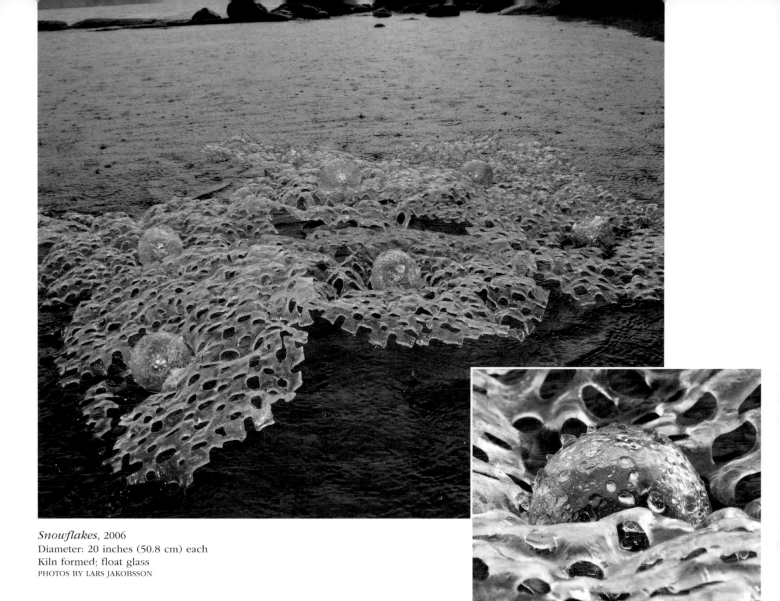

Snowflakes, 2006
Diameter: 20 inches (50.8 cm) each
Kiln formed; float glass
PHOTOS BY LARS JAKOBSSON

ty in the ecosystems of nature, as well as the vulnerability and sometimes painful experience of being human, are issues I work with, and they inform the questions I try to ask. It has come to pass, in the fullness of time, that I see the light of human beings and their brittleness as also connected to the qualities of glass. For me, glass is the medium for the spiritual side of life.

During the three decades I've been working with glass, my works have become increasingly fragile. I think my interest in projects and pieces about the relationship of man, culture, and nature has played a big part in that development. In this process of dialogue with nature, glass is my companion in everyday life. So, I have found my garden and life itself to be my most immediate and powerful sources of inspiration.

THE FLAME AND THE KILN

Like that of other members of the studio-glass movement in Sweden during the late 1960s and early 1970s, my relationship with glass had its roots in clay. Somewhere along the way, glass came into my life. My challenge was to develop an approach to the material more free than the strong Swedish traditions for handling glass suggested. Those traditions were reflected in the work at the factories in the Swedish "glass kingdom"—the glass district of Småland.

I admire the old, beautiful craft traditions of Swedish glassblowing. At the factories, the masters, whose magical creations glow on their blowpipes, teach students how to produce goblets and bowls. Encountering the noises and the smells here, and witnessing with my own eyes these strong men

Ingalena Klenell

Fragrance of the Sky, 2003
196 x 81 inches (497.8 x 205.7 cm)
Kiln formed; float glass
PHOTOS BY GUDRUN HAGERO

Couple, 2000
48 x 12 inches (121.9 x 30.5 cm)
Kiln formed, crocheted; float glass
PHOTO BY RAGNAR KLENELL

3 Cylinders I, 2004
48 x 12 inches (121.9 x 30.5 cm)
Kiln formed; float glass
PHOTO BY RAGNAR KLENELL

playing with fire and mastering it, was like seeing a manifestation of Eros. I wanted to dance in that energy.

Even when I went to the National School of Glass in Orrefors, Sweden, to learn how to blow glass, I wasn't kiln forming yet. Using a torch in flamework is still not a very common technique in Sweden.

My husband, Ragnar Klenell, and I moved to Edsbjörke to build our studio in 1978. Edsbjörke is situated in the western part of Sweden. At this time, I started to experiment with cold glass in a small kiln. Although we had spent some years in Gothenburg blowing glass, I was always searching for something else.

By chance, I received the glass and all the equipment from a studio owned by a man who had worked on stained-glass windows for churches. This man had a big collection of the most beautiful glass—sheets of glass, most of them hand blown, with overlays and underlays in the most wonderful colors and combinations. Many boxes of scrap glass and tools for cutting were a part of the fantastic gift from this man to me.

I started to experiment with this glass. At the time, I had no knowledge about how to create a kiln firing schedule. I often overfired the glass, because I was used to melting recycled bottles and window glass. I spent one year with a kiln that had an instrument that could only indicate the kiln temperature. My relationship to this kiln became a technical dialogue about top temperatures, annealing, the length of holding times needed, and all the problems surrounding how to use the kiln for different purposes. (This was before my first kiln for fusing, which was supplied with a computer for exact firings, was built—very luxurious for me!)

I work with several different glass techniques, including flameworking, hot casting, kiln forming, blowing, and kiln casting. Comparing flameworking and kiln forming is intriguing to me. I've found that when I work with the torch, I'm like the computer on the kiln. Like that computer, I am a tool receiving a lot of information through my senses, and I must be present to operate correctly. Kiln forming, by contrast, involves a lot of thinking, and I work at a distance from the glass.

Flameworking is a wonderful occupation for me. I must be present in my body, in the same way as when I skate on the ice. Flameworking is a transitional experience; it opens the door to the field of my imagination and starts the creative process. Melting a clear glass rod in the flame, and at the same time letting go of the tensions in my body, is meditation. Flameworking provides a meditative experience that separates me out from the production work I have to do to make my living and from the other kinds of work I do in the studio. To flamework is to relax.

Kiln forming means working at more of a distance from the elements. First, I have to break down a sheet of glass to build a new structure. I start by creating chaos in order to make form. Kiln forming is more about working with shadows that strengthen and tell us about light.

Using the torch is a powerful way to go into something beyond the self. It opens me up to the impressions of the psyche that lie out of my reach during my ordinary daily routines. Flamework puts

Spine, 1999
18½ x 25 inches (47 x 63.5 cm)
Kiln formed; float glass
PHOTO BY RAGNAR KLENELL

Ingalena Klenell

me in a state of mind that is somewhere "in between"—what's sometimes called a "liminal space." In this space, images, memories, sensations, and sources of knowledge are hidden away, safe from the analytic, censoring mind. It's like a treasury of ideas.

Art making is meditation—a joyful state of consciousness in which the nonrational, intuitive qualities of imagination join together with the subconscious. A bridge forms between our inner life and vision and our outer expression in the world. To see children at play is fascinating and inspiring and has its roots in this same place. Children's irrepressible creativity and spontaneous brilliance have been formative in the most profound artistic changes in my development. I think this has to do with paying attention to the aspect of joy and imagination in the artistic process, and with the fact that children are naturally closer to authentic expressions.

Mandala, 2003
33 inches (83.8 cm)
Kiln formed; decal, float glass
PHOTO BY RAGNAR KLENELL

WOMEN WITH NEEDLES AND TORCHES

My work may be seen as primarily sculptural, but it's inspired by folk art and craft. I like to compare my relationship to the torch to my grandmother's crocheting. The clear glass is like her ball of white yarn; it melts and becomes smaller and smaller. Like her, I build nets with my material—glass—and somehow my glass creations are more fragile than her crocheted ones.

Like many women who lived in the countryside, my grandmother crocheted beautiful tablecloths, curtains, and bedspreads. Her pieces were the most beautiful of all of them, at least seen through my eyes as a child. She taught me to crochet when I was seven years old. Her patience was impressed upon me and transferred to me. My grandmother would create many small units, such as squares or stars, and collect them in a basket to be put together into a big piece.

When I first saw an installation by Japanese glass artist Harumi Yukatake, at the Corning Incorporated headquarters building in Corning, New York, I got the same feeling I had when my grandmother made crafts for her family and friends. Yukatake created a repeated form that became something that expressed a monumental presence. Her big construction, made from many small, interchangeable units, had a great impact on me. Each piece of glass caught the light, and the whole sculpture shimmered.

Beauty is interpreted in that artwork with a presence and precision that still really touches me. My grandmother also was present and surrounded by a shimmer of light as she sat with her crochet, light falling in from the window.

I think light is the deepest aspect of beauty.

Anna Skibska's big, fragile glass sculptures also give me that feeling. Skibska's work is monumental and simple, without practical compromises, and I'm inspired by the bravery of her artistic vision. Beauty never tells me anything about what I shall do in life, but in the moment of its touch, I know that I'm not alone.

As an artist, I've been investigating women's creativity by trying to translate my grandmother's work in glass. Her big bedspreads inspired me to try to translate them into hanging glass star cloths and cylinders that remind me of crochet. It was interesting for me to try to touch my grandmother and imagine what she could have felt. She was a very graceful woman, as I remember her, and that was very important for me as a child. After a hard day at the farm, she sat down with her handicraft, and I think she found, through her form of artistic meditation, the peaceful state she needed to endure another working day at the farm.

I kiln form float glass and use the diamond in the glass cutter as my needle. I use float glass because it gives me a half-transparent surface when I take it to 1508°F to 1517°F (820°C to 825°C) and hold it there for 20 minutes.

Sometimes I wonder if my grandmother dreamed about being somewhere else in the world or in another time, just as the dreams about a historical woman have occupied me. The holy saint Birgitta lived in Sweden before she left for Rome. There was a celebration in Sweden in 2003, on her 700th birthday. Birgitta wrote about her extraordinary revelations. She had a revelation when she lived in Rome that led her to build a cathedral in her hometown, Vadstena. Her daughter fulfilled that vision when she came back to Sweden after her mother died.

For an exhibition during the Birgitta celebration, I made the cathedral in glass as a hanging coat in a cross form, with an open cylinder people can walk into.

The circle—often in the form of mandalas—is something I've been coming back to regularly in my work. I create cylinders of different sizes in the work about my grandmother and the mandalas inspired by the Tibetans in Dharamsala, India, and in Nepal. I've seen very complicated crafts and compositions made in Dharamsala, which is the center of Tibetan culture today. I have also seen beautiful, folklore-inspired work in Nepal. All this fantastic art has a mainly spiritual purpose—it is created for spiritual development. Tibetan art is a wonderful, beautiful example of how to step into the liminal space; art serves as the imaginative tool in a powerful ritual that has the aim of reaching an experience of wholeness.

Large-scale work fascinates me. I like to communicate with—and then communicate about—the different places that I visit and the

Circles of Emptiness, 2004
Diameter: 39 inches (99.1 cm) each
Kiln formed; float glass
PHOTOS BY RAGNAR KLENELL

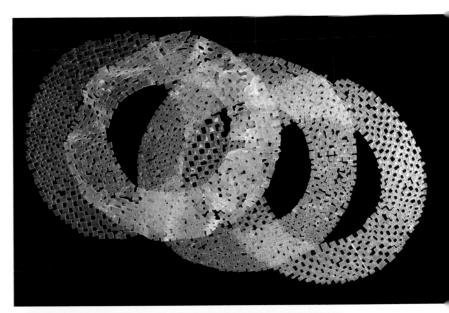

rooms in which I make my installations. The brittle qualities of glass—reflected in light and transparency—have always been important to what I'm expressing in my work, but now I also see the shadows that appear when light is there as being part of my artistic vision.

To work is to communicate in time and space, and glass is the very best medium for crystallizing what I want to communicate—the existential vulnerability, brittleness, and eminent light of the human condition.

Hands On

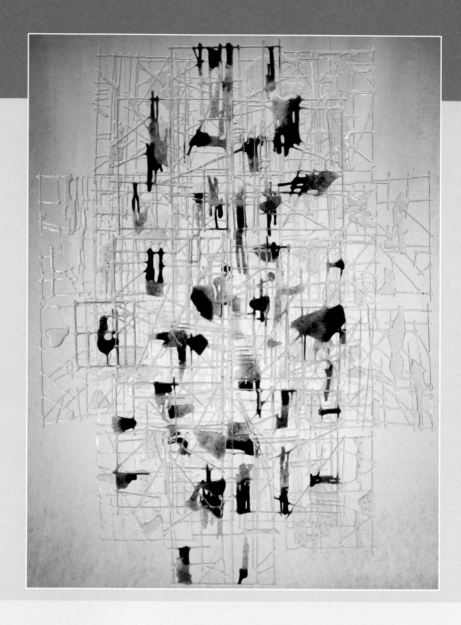

Ingalena Klenell says, "I use kiln forming as a complement to my flamework, so I'm choosing to use my how-to section to demonstrate the versatile techniques I employ with the kiln as I create a large sculpture called Landscape and Memory. The piece is inspired by how human memories are created as narratives from different places—both from our psyches and from different geographical spaces in the outer world."

1 The project is made with clear rods. A friend once called up and offered me five tons of them. This glass contains a lot of borax, and it has a green tone that I like.

2 Here's my studio, as I carry the long, clear rods into it.

Ingalena Klenell

4 I start to cut the glass rods with pliers. When I find a length I like, I measure subsequent cuts against it, or against sample forms I've already put together; I made the glass "sketches" shown here with the torch. I need a lot of cut rods to fill the kiln.

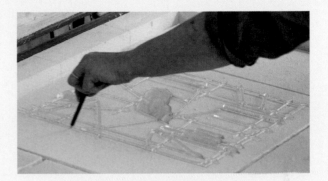

3 This project requires a kiln big enough to give me a clear overview of all the lines I'm going to make. My fusing kiln is used for flat kiln-forming projects. The kiln's flat surface is 7 feet 2 inches by 3 feet 7 inches (2.2 by 1.1 m), and it has 16 inches (0.4 m) of vertical room. I prepare the shelves with kiln wash. To do this, I use simple dry kaolin, a fine clay that gives an interesting pattern. I sift the kaolin onto the shelves with a little teaball—a very effective tool.

5 I use my sample form to roughly trace the form in the kiln. These marks will show me about where to put the rods to build the piece up.

6 I start to put rods into the kiln.

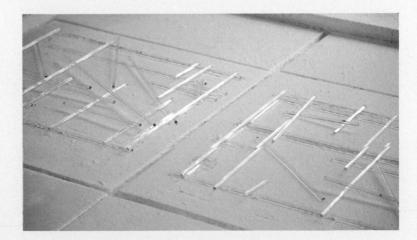

7 This step looks and even feels like a game; as the rods are built up, many are balanced on one another.

Ingalena Klenell

8 Part of the construction involves making the areas of the piece that portray the landscape. These are made in another kiln by fusing together rods of different sizes. I use a full-fuse program—I fuse the rods at a temperature that results in my no longer being able to see the individual rods. This type of glass is soft and has a full-fuse temperature of 1438°F (781°C).

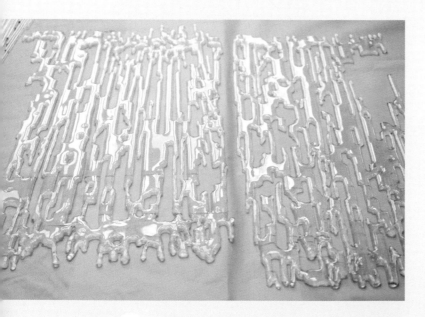

9 Now totally melted together, the kiln-fused glass has interesting holes and openings in it.

10 I want to have interesting shapes that look like they've been shaped by nature or visualized as if on a map, so I break the fused glass with a hammer to give the landscape pieces this organic form.

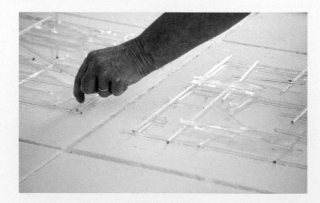

11 I choose the landscape pieces I like and arrange them on the rod frameworks in the bigger kiln.

12 It's very important to have precise control over what happens in the kiln. I take notes on every experiment I conduct so that I can find the exact firing program for the results I want. The notes taken during each firing are fantastic sources of information for subsequent firings. They help determine the firing requirements for subtly different types of glass and for projects that include different sizes and thicknesses of glass.

For this project, I have learned where to set the top temperature for a full fuse and also for the annealing point, which is so important for the work. Because this project has only one layer of glass in the kiln, which is not more than 1³⁄₁₆ to 1⁹⁄₁₆ inches (3 to 4 cm) thick, I can use a short firing schedule.

To fully fuse the rods, I increase the temperature by about 108°F (60°C) per hour until the kiln reaches 250°F (120°C); I do not want the small, light glass rods to jump due to the heat. I need to increase the temperature to pass the annealing point, which for this quality of glass is 930°F (500°C), so I increase the temperature again by about 360°F (200°C) per hour until the kiln reaches 970°F (520°C).

As fast as possible, I increase to a top temperature of 1470°F (800°C), and I hold for 15 minutes at the top. Next, again as fast as possible, I go down to the annealing point of 930°F (500°C). I hold there for 100 minutes, which is the amount of time I use when I make things that do not need a very exact determination—I just want to be sure they're properly annealed. To be even more certain, I go down by 90°F (50°C) per hour until I reach 650°F (345°C) and then let the temperature go down by ending the program.

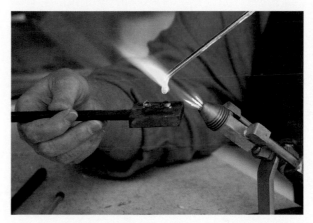

13 I want to include many small glass dots to portray the fragments we carry in our psyches—all in different parts of the brain, all from different periods in our lives. I flamework them on the torch by melting rods and dripping the resulting little dots on the marver.

14 Using the kiln, I will tack fuse all these dots onto the pieces in the construction.

Ingalena Klenell

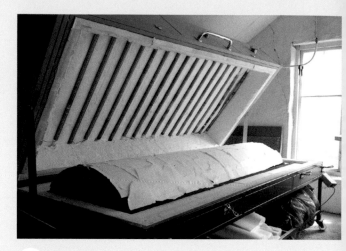

15 I prepare the large kiln again with kaolin, put the pieces back in, and place the small dots on the landscape pieces. Tack fusing in the kiln glues the dots onto the glass surfaces.

5. Decrease by 90°F (50°C) per hour to 650°F (345°C). End the program, and let the glass cool.

17 Now most of my components for *Landscape and Memory* are created. I still have to bend the pieces that I'll be placing on the sides. To do this, I make a mold using a ⅛-inch-thick (3 mm) sheet of iron. I make a frame of angled iron to hold the mold up, and I also support it with bricks. I cover the mold with ceramic paper; it also can be powdered with kaolin.

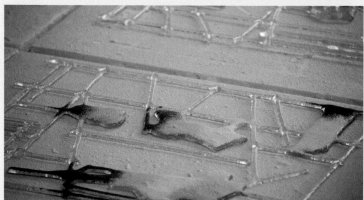

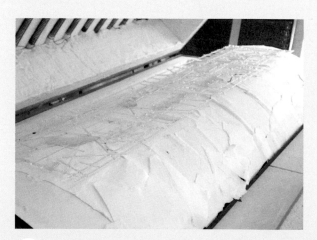

16 I "paint" some of the landscape pieces by sifting glass powder onto the glass with the little teaball sifter.

Here's my firing schedule for the dots and paint:
1. Increase by 108°F (60°C) per hour to 250°F (120°C).
2. Increase by 360°F (200°C) per hour to 970°F (520°C).
3. Increase as fast as possible to 1260°F (680°C) and hold for 15 minutes.
4. Decrease as fast as possible down to the annealing point of 930°F (500°C) and hold for 100 minutes.

18 I place the pieces that I'll be slumping on the mold and slump them with this firing schedule:
1. Increase by 108°F (60°C) per hour to 250°F (120°C).
2. Increase by 360°F (200°C) per hour to 970°F (520°C).
3. Increase as fast as possible to 1190°F (640°C) and hold for 10 minutes.
4. Decrease as fast as possible to the annealing point of 930°F (500°C) and hold for 100 minutes.
5. Decrease by 90°F (50°C) per hour to 650°F (345°C). End the firing, and let the glass cool.

19 These pieces have been slumped in the kiln.

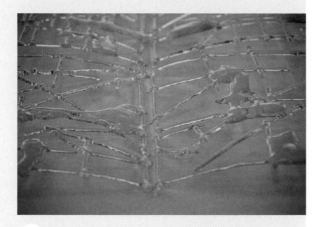

20 The side pieces—bent from the firing on the mold—will be placed on the sides of the construction. I use wire to attach the pieces to one another and to hang them from the ceiling.

Ingalena Klenell has been working with glass since 1976. She and her husband, Ragnar Klenell, built a studio in Edsbjörke, Sunne, in the Värmland region of western Sweden. Ingalena started out with glassblowing and developed her glasswork by researching and fusing colored glass made for windows and stained-glass applications. She uses glass to build up elements that are kiln formed; then flameworked parts are tack fused onto the fired glass. Her large-scale work is designed for installation so that it can be part of the dialogue of man and nature. She sometimes creates works for municipal buildings and other places where she can communicate with the surrounding environment.

Ingalena says she wants to express the light and vulnerability of life in her work. She finds glass to be the best medium for projects about nature and existence. The beautiful landscape of the area in which she lives and her dialogue with it are her most important sources of inspiration. She studied ecophilosophy at Karlstad University; she has a master's degree in environmental science and ecophilosophy. She learned to work glass at the National School of Glass, in Orrefors, Sweden, and she learned about light, as well as about architectural lighting design, at KTH School of Technology and Health in Stockholm.

Ingalena has exhibited her work widely in Europe and the United States. She and her husband hold workshops in their studio, where international artists are invited to teach and meet Swedish artists. She has also taught at UrbanGlass in Brooklyn, New York, and Konstfack University College of Arts, Crafts and Design in Stockholm. Since 2002, she and American artist Beth Lipman have taught collaboratively at The Studio of The Corning Museum of Glass in Corning, New York; Penland School of Crafts in Penland, North Carolina; Pittsburgh Glass Center in Pittsburgh, Pennsylvania; and Worcester Center for Crafts in Worcester, Massachusetts.

Eva's Spheres, 2007
78 x 78 inches (198.1 x 198.1 cm)
Blown, cast, slumped; soda-lime glass
PHOTO BY RAGNAR KLENELL

Susan Plum

A bicultural Mesoamerican perspective and a fascination with the universal interconnectedness of all things inform Susan Plum's glass weavings and installations. Susan's experiments in other media help her to achieve a wider artistic expression as she translates her designs into other forms. Sometimes complex, always compelling, her work comments on political and social conditions, as well as the human condition.

Candelabra, 2001
22 x 26 inches (55.9 x 66 cm)
Flameworked; borosilicate glass
PHOTO BY LEE FATHEREE

Across the Woven Universe

Nature in all its intrinsic beauty and alchemical force has been the driving influence in my work. I have researched the universe's creation myths and the elemental forces of fire, air, earth, and water, and I've been captivated by the awesomeness of the sky bodies, nebulae, cosmic knots, and superstring theory. This may sound like a huge range of information to traverse, but to me it all speaks to the wonder of nature.

In the 1980s, I took my first class at Pilchuck Glass School in Stanwood, Washington. Ginny Ruffner was my teacher, and I felt that I had discovered my missing link—flameworked glass. So many elements came into play—fire, air, and glass (in the role of water)—in a mesmerizing dance of light, fluidity, and flame. Flamework allowed me to weave layer upon layer of glass in order to reveal a story conceptually and through a play of light.

I became a teacher's assistant at Pilchuck Glass School and then a teacher there myself. I went on to start the flameworking department, which at the time consisted of one torch, at Pratt Fine Arts Center in Seattle. I was making glass sculpture, using heavier glass than I now use. By the 1990s I had my own studio and kiln. I taught at Pilchuck; then Penland School of Crafts in Penland, North Carolina; and later The Studio of the Corning Museum of Glass in Corning, New York.

Teaching at Penland was a memorable experience, because the school's environment encourages collaboration and community. It was my great pleasure to become close friends with Paulus Berensohn. Our mutual recognition in each other and the language of our work continues to be a blessing and inspiration for me.

In 1992, I started making installations rather than just focusing on sculpture. Most of my ideas come from reading or a visual trigger that connects synergistically with an earlier idea. Sometimes the concept and visual component are brought together in a flash. At other times, it's more a matter of waiting for information to gather and begin to take form. It

Falling Bodies Taking Flight, 1992
Various dimensions
Flameworked; hazel tree branches, borosilicate glass branches, fresh oranges
PHOTOS BY LEE FATHEREE

Susan Plum

may take up to a year or two before the information is fully integrated and the actual work begins.

Sacred Garden: An Invocation to the Heart and *Falling Bodies Taking Flight*, two separate installations that exhibited simultaneously in 1992, are good examples. As I began processing information for these installations, I saw in my mind's eye a pyramid of fresh oranges. Through research, I learned that the orange has many layers of historical and mythological meanings. The divergent meanings of the orange in Eastern and Western mythologies became the basis for the installations.

Sacred Garden: Invocation to the Heart was conceived as a celestial garden and had the more formal presentation of the two. *Falling Bodies Taking Flight* was the more lyrical installation: Oranges hanging from the ceiling were the celestial fruit. Below the oranges, flameworked glass limbs were interwoven with hazel tree limbs. Walking into the darkened room and seeing the floating oranges created a feeling of suspended time. A sense of movement and a sense of stillness coexisted, as though the viewer were about to encounter an astronomical event. The oranges—a symbol of the fruit of the Fall and of Eve, the fallen woman—had taken flight. Free of restriction, they joined with the stars and planets.

Tejido I (Weavings), 1997
35 x 19½ inches (88.9 x 49.5 cm)
Flameworked; borosilicate glass
PHOTO BY LEE FATHEREE

COSMIC VISIONS

I would have adopted the weaving method for flameworked glass much earlier, but I did not discover the thin glass rods I use until 1995. I weave these glass rods into patterned webs or multilayered aggregations that both reflect and concentrate light. They are simultaneously transparent and yet impenetrable, much like the numinous centers of the great nebulae that have also become powerful influences in my work.

My series *Tejidos*, which I began in 1997, is an homage to the Mayan goddess Ixchel, the first weaver of the Americas. *Tejido I* (*Weavings*) was my first work made exclusively of woven glass. The Maya thought of the weaver's loom as a metaphor for the universe. The vessel is the central shape and vehicle that I used to tell Ixchel's story, which is related to both astronomy and healing. She is a lunar goddess and healer to all women, and the dragonfly is her symbol of magic. The numerous sculptures that comprise the *Tejidos* series progress from *Tejido I* (*Weavings*)—a simple vessel shape signifying the pupa stage—to *Tejido XIII* (*Weavings*), which represents the final stage of transformation into a dragonfly.

For me, flameworking is a fairly simple technique. I typically use ¹⁄₁₆- to ⅛-inch (2 to 3 mm) borosilicate glass rods; by contrast, working with thicker glass requires the use of a kiln and much more technical knowledge. I find that working with thick glass also keeps me stuck in one place. By using thin rods, which do not require a kiln, I can work wherever I go—all I need is oxygen, propane, glass, and a torch.

Breakage is minimal in my work, and replacing a broken area simply means rebuilding it. Structural strength is the most important consideration. In the *Tejidos* series, for example, I constructed large glass armatures in order to ensure the support of all the layers, which was essential to maintaining the integrity of these particular sculptures.

When I first found glass, it grounded my vision. Glass brings me a sense of wonder, and it signifies the element of light to me. Carl Jung described glass as solidified water, signifying spirit. To be

Susan Plum

Tejido VII (Weavings), 1997
33 x 21 x 21 inches (83.8 x 53.3 x 53.3 cm)
Flameworked; borosilicate glass
PHOTOS BY LEE FATHEREE

Tejido XIII (Weavings), 1997
35 x 54 x 12 inches (88.9 x 137.2 x 30.5 cm)
Flameworked; borosilicate glass
PHOTO BY LEE FATHEREE

Susan Plum

sure, glass is one of the most mysterious materials available to us. I've heard some scientists say that they study glass because it's the material that most closely resembles the "glue" that holds the universe together.

In the cosmology of the Maya, the universe is actually a construction on a huge loom. The heavens and Earth are woven from filaments of light. When the strands of light become tangled, discord on Earth results. The task of entering into the other dimensions and untangling the tangled cords falls to the Mayan shamans. To the Maya, the acts of weaving and untangling are the equivalents of building and re-energizing the world.

While simultaneously researching cosmic mathematical knots, mystical knots, string theory, and nebulae, I began to see the connection between the cosmic knots and the nebulae. I created a body of work—half of which consisted of glass wall sculptures—that to me resembled the nebulae, and incorporated the strings and mathematical knots as well. I saw these pieces as enormous flowers in the sky. The other half of the work was embroideries that replicated the glass sculptures, creating a dialogue between each sculpture and embroidered piece. I also began to notice that human sensory organs seemed to appear within the cosmic bodies, or nebulae, that I was researching and creating, which brought up the question of the role nebulae play in the cosmological story, at least as seen through my artist's vision. Are these nebulae in some way the sensory organs of the universe?

In the Aztec cosmic vision, the coming age is called the Age of Flowers (*Tonatiuh Xochitl*). This time will bring a deeper understanding of intrinsic beauty and sensuality, a more profound knowledge, and an opening up of the senses. The Aztecs believe that there will be a cross-pollination—an enhanced communication and interchange— between cosmic bodies and the Earth, as well as a more unified spiritual belief system.

My nebulae paintings evolved from my work with the glass nebulae and knots for my show *Knots and Nebulae*. I now see myself as recording the nebulae, or cosmic language, by first "drawing" with glass—a molten, gaseous, transparent material—and then photographing the finished glass

Intersection, 2007
65 x 62 inches (165.1 x 157.5 cm)
Flameworked; borosilicate glass, natural Fichus tree, acrylic paint, kiln shelves, mixed media
PHOTO BY RAY CARRINGTON

piece, printing it, and transferring it onto a mixed-media board; I describe this process in my Hands On section. In this way, my work is not unlike a telescope with a camera that photographs the sky bodies, documenting the information so that we can print it out in order to "see" what the telescope is seeing. For me, glass concretizes the invisible!

Susan Plum

Borderscapes, 1999
Flameworked; natural branch, borosilicate
glass, cast wax, metal
PHOTO BY ARTIST
INSTALLATION WITH JOYCE SCOTT

BICULTURALISM AND ART ACTIVISM

I was raised in Mexico City, left Mexico for the
United States in 1965 at age twenty, and moved
back in 2003 to settle in San Miguel de Allende, so
I am no longer cutting off a part of myself. San
Miguel allows me more of a bicultural integration
than my U.S. homes did. It has been very healing
to rediscover more consciously my dual nature.

The move back to Mexico has changed my art,
too, through the wonderful working relationships I
have developed with talented artisans. For instance,
I've worked with young women from the countryside who make a living embroidering while they
stay at home to care for their children. The work
we've done together includes the embroideries for
the exhibit *Knots and Nebulae*, in which I replicated on linen the flameworked glass sculptures I'd
created.

Twice I have unexpectedly met young artisans
on the street who subsequently became involved
with my work. One day I came across a young
man sitting on the curb caning chairs. I asked if he
would be interested in helping me make some
brooms. Without hesitation, he followed me home
to discuss the project. After a few tries, Teo, his
brother Alberto, and I succeeded in making the
imposing 14-foot (4.3 meter) brooms for my installation *Luz y Solidaridad* (*Light and Solidarity*).

In another instance, I asked a cab driver if he
knew of any stained-glass artisans. The moment he
answered that he did, a motorcycle came toward
us—driven by the very stained-glass person he was
thinking of! Although San Miguel is a small town,
this kind of magic occurs far too often for simple
explanations to suffice.

The *Luz y Solidaridad (Light and Solidarity)* installation in Queretaro, Mexico, in February 2006 featured a wordless ritual by women who included mothers of some of Ciudad Juárez's slain girls and women, a flameworked bronze tree, cast wax figures, photographs, grinding stones made of carved volcanic rocks, and black plastic brooms.

PHOTOS BY OCTAVIO RODRIGUEZ

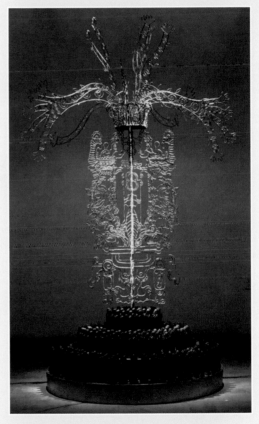

Susan Plum

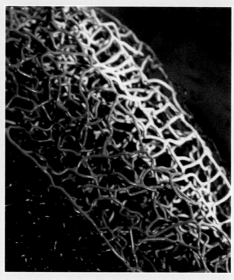

Corazon de la Tierra (Heart of the Earth), 2007
34 x 34 inches (86.4 x 86.4 cm)
Flameworked; mixed media on board, borosilicate
glass, charcoal, enamel spray paint
PHOTOS BY LANDER RODRIGUEZ

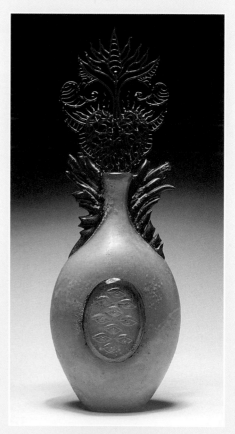

Remedio Mandragora, 2001
30 x 26 x 10 inches (76.2 x 66 x 25.4 cm)
Flameworked, blown, cast; glass, glass lacquer, spray enamel
PHOTO BY LEE FATHEREE

Remedio Amarillo (Yellow Remedy), 1999
33 x 14 x 9 inches (83.8 x 35.6 x 22.9 cm)
Flameworked, blown, cast; glass, glass lacquer,
spray enamel
PHOTO BY LEE FATHEREE

Living in Mexico has expanded my vision and given me the opportunity to work with highly skilled artisans who have enriched my life and work immensely. Coming home to the land of my childhood—the country I love so much—has nourished and inspired me. Back in 1999, I became aware of a long, massive, and horrific string of murders of young women and girls in Ciudad Juárez, Mexico. The Ciudad Juárez events will probably never see justice. Although the resulting installation did not involve flameworked glass, I think it's helpful in understanding my artistic vision and my work. I am an artist-activist who believes that art transforms.

In 2004 I met with Marisela Ortíz Rivera, head of the organization Nuestras Hijas de Regreso a Casa (May Our Daughters Return Home). She introduced me to several mothers who had lost daughters. In response, I designed an installation and performance ritual that included the participation of the bereaved mothers, in the hope that this would give them a sense of empowerment. The installation and performance ritual *Luz y Solidaridad* (*Light and Solidarity*) honors the families, and particularly the mothers, of the 450 young women and girls who have been murdered and the 600 who have disappeared in Ciudad Juárez over more than a decade.

Luz y Solidaridad (*Light and Solidarity*) initially began as a call to action—for people to light votive candles with the intention of bringing light to the murdered daughters and solidarity to the mothers. More than 400 people from around the world responded by sending photographs, which became part of the installation.

The installation and performance ritual opened at the Museo de la Ciudad in Querétaro, Mexico, in February 2006. The wordless ritual was performed in an open-air courtyard adjacent to the exhibition, prior to the opening of the installation. Twenty-five Mexican and American women, including three of the bereaved mothers, used the sound and movement of brooms, pre-Hispanic wind whistles, bullroarers, and spinners to perform a *limpia*, or shamanic cleansing.

I believe I was five or six years old when the painted trees in Mexico City came into my conscious line of vision. I was stunned! People actually *painted* trees. I came home; found the "red medicine," or merthiolate (a ferocious, wonderful, red, day-glowish medicine); and painted my chest of drawers. The experience of being bicultural has always influenced how I view the world. I think I see it from a place "in-between."

Since returning to Mexico, I am better able to understand what this means to me, and I try to capture the understanding in work such as my installation *Intersection*. In 2005, while I was working on the Querétaro installation, I was entranced once again by painted trees. A *zócalo*—a square with cafés and shops—was surrounded by beautiful ficus trees partially painted white. The paint on the trees shifted my perspective yet again. The trees became a metaphor for paradox, duality, biculturalism, borders, liminal states, self and other, and racial demarcation. The trees looked human-like to me, with a gentleness, a tolerance, and a capacity to contain diversity, paradox, and duality.

The political, social, violent, and ecologically unbalanced climate that prevails in the world today emphasizes difference, disunity, and destruction, rather than the qualities of unity and creativity that I believe reflect productive, constructive energy. The DNA-shaped ficus tree in *Intersection* speaks to this unity. The roots and branches are woven with thin glass rods that represent light and a promise for change.

There is beauty in the world, always. Myth and science both reveal that deep within destruction reside the animating forces of the universe. As an artist, I look toward nature's self-generation, self-restoration, and renewal. Both in content and process, I express in my work patterns of integration, healing, and ultimately wholeness.

Hands On

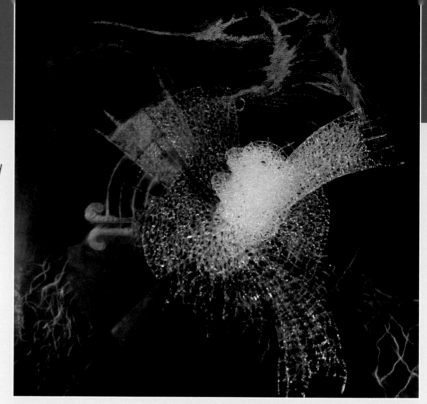

Susan Plum demonstrates how she weaves glass around armatures and also how she transfers her glass designs onto other media.

In 2006, astronomers using observations from NASA's Spitzer Space Telescope reported the sighting of an elongated DNA-shaped double helix nebula near the center of the Milky Way—our own Galactic Center. Because this nebula is magnetically and physically connected to the galactic center in the way described by ancient Mesoamerican astronomers, it seems undeniable to me that the Maya had their fingers on the pulse of contemporary science and cosmology.

Corazon del Cielo (Heart of Heaven), the piece I am creating in the first part of my Hands On section, was inspired by the Mayan glyph for our Galactic Center. The woven-glass double helix rises out of the Galactic Center as though reaching for a new intelligence. A black background with white chalk drawings, as well as the shape of the glass weaving, evoke a sense of centrifugal movement. A sister piece—they are exhibited together—is *Corazon de la Tierra (Heart of Earth)*, which is featured on page 202 and has a red background with black charcoal drawings. The red background and black drawings represent an overheated earth, both physically and emotionally.

1 Oxygen and propane are used to heat the glass. The cardboard boxes in this photo are 25-pound (11.3 kg) cases of ¹⁄₁₆- to ⅛-inch (2 to 3 mm) borosilicate glass rods. In my opinion, this thin glass does not require annealing (although I know many artists would disagree), so when I am creating installations I can do flamework on-site, if I choose.

Susan Plum

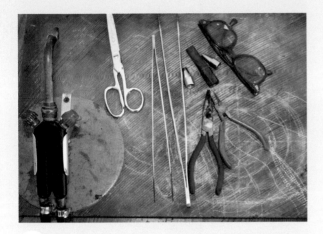

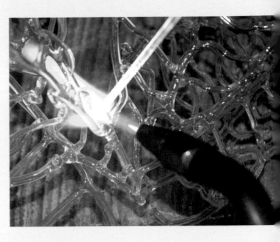

4 Here I'm adding a glass rod, heating and forming its shape. I then fuse the glass. It's essential that borosilicate glass be fully fused so that it melts into itself. In the absence of a full fuse, stress, fragility, and breakage will result.

2 Because I use such thin glass, I need minimal tools. Tweezers and a torch with my preferred tip are basically all I need. I use a size 2 tip unless I am working on a large installation. I wear safety glasses, and pliers and scissors sometimes come in handy.

3 Fire and air are the elements that bring the glass to life. When the torch and glass gather enough heat, the color is very intense. At that moment, it's beautiful to see the light traveling down the rod of glass.

When I'm working with these glass rods, I feel as if I'm weaving with filaments of light. It's no wonder I spend so much time in the cosmic realms. For me, the cosmic realms and the deep infrastructure of nature both have the same visual language, in the same way that creation myths speak of both macrocosm and microcosm.

5 I start off by making concentric circles. I then attach rods oriented perpendicularly to the base. I build a temporary supporting armature of cube-like structures to hold and support the glass weaving as I work. I weave between the perpendicular rods.

Susan Plum

6 The armature for this piece does not have to be very large, but for some pieces I've made armatures up to 6 square feet (.56 square meters) in size in order to support the glass as I work it.

9 I add glass to the concentric circles and weave between the perpendicular rods, navigating between those rods and the armature. When the glass is this densely woven, it can take about 18 hours to weave about 5 square inches (32.3 square centimeters).

7 The larger the armature, the trickier it gets. Rods this thin tend to move easily, and I often end up chasing the rod with the flame! Finishing the armature is the most intense part of the work and the part that requires the most engineering.

8 The armature is completed. In some cases, I have to build the armature as I go, adding more volume or angles depending on the requirements of the work.

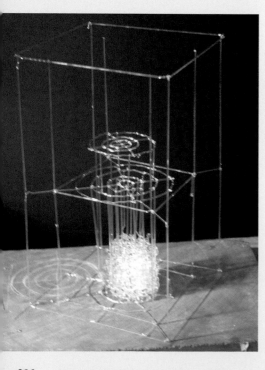

10 The core shape I'm making—the main focus of the piece—is a three-dimensional double helix. Here it's completed. I remove the armature, which is no longer needed, by heating and detaching the rods. Now my work gets exciting: I need to assess how I've brought the idea into cohesive form, visually and conceptually. How's it going to work? Do I need to create more—and perhaps another armature—to create a desired effect? I've titled the piece *Corazon del Cielo (Heart of Heaven)*. It relates to the center of our galaxy, so there needs to be a sense of motion and force.

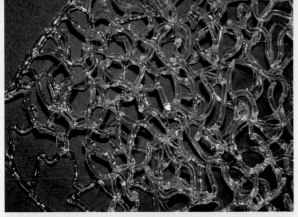

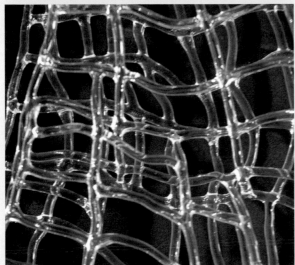

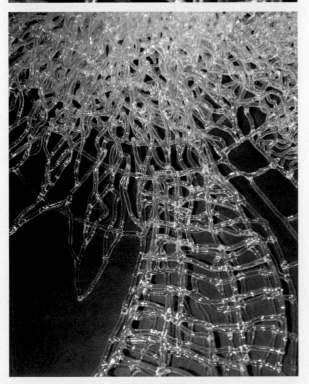

11 Weaving the fabric of the universe! What an opportunity to imagine such a beautiful thing. I use ⅛-inch (3 mm) glass to add weight to the "fabric." I add more circles and weave more protruding waves to add to the flow and motion of the piece.

12 I paint a 34 by 34 inch (86.4 by 86.4 cm) board with blackboard paint and draw on it with chalk and pastel. I've made a metal armature to attach the glass ¾ inch (1.9 cm) away from the board. This added depth contributes to the sense of motion. When the work is lit properly, shadows from the glass fall onto the background, creating more mystery and dimension.

13 My woven glass pieces stand on their own, of course, but they also provide fodder for sister designs in other media. Sometimes I use a piece already created, and at other times I make flameworked glass forms—again, using ¹⁄₁₆- to ⅛-inch (2 to 3 mm) borosilicate glass rods—with the specific intention of using them for making the paintings. My pieces can take several days to several weeks to create. I am essentially drawing with the glass.

The piece is digitally photographed and downloaded onto my computer. I invert the glass image into a black-and-white print.

Susan Plum

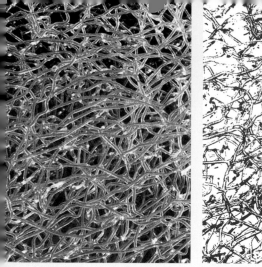
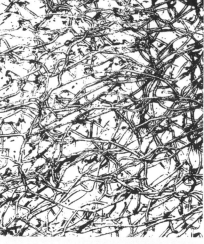

14 Here's a "before and after": my detail photo of a woven-glass piece and the inversion of the photo using a popular graphics-editor software program.

17 A print is placed upside down onto the prepared board. I rub its reverse side with a solvent until the image has been transferred onto the board. After lifting the print, the same process continues—I can use repetition or layering or add other drawings until my painting is complete. All the preparation—making the flameworked glass pieces and photographing, downloading, and copying them—comes together at this point to create a sense of anticipation, discovery, and creative wonder.

15 Here's another example: My blown, cast, and flameworked glass piece *Remedio Divino* has been converted into a black-and-white print. Modern printers offer endless possibilities for reducing or enlarging copies, as well as for repetition and layering.

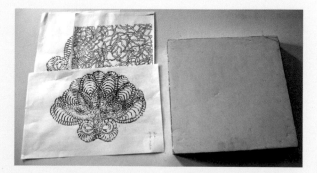

16 I use a spatula to cover a board, which will be my canvas, with a variety of mediums. After it has dried, I sand it, leaving some of the texture.

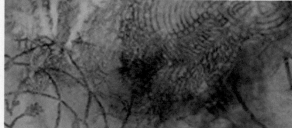

18 Cosmic knots, mathematical knots, marine knots, and mystical knots make up part of the language of my paintings. I copy and transfer images, and sometimes draw new ones with a quill. I maintain a large, flat file filled with copies of glass pieces and knots—a real treasure-trove of images that I can work with whenever I need them. This painting is called *Naruraleza Oculta—Hidden Nature.*

19 After I feel that a drawing is complete, I bring in color by using paint, mostly gouache and small amounts of acrylic. I use a quill pen and India ink for outlining, drawing, and accenting shapes. The process of getting the painting to take shape is more about taking away than it is about adding. The drawings are transferred, and then I might sand some of the areas. I add the gouache and then rub it to take away some of the color. I add more, take away more, and so on, until the painting has just the right layers to create a mysterious atmosphere of line, color, and shape. Pictured here is the painting *Naturaleza Oculta—Hidden Nature II.*

Susan Plum was one of many children of American parents raised in Mexico City, one of the great, sophisticated cultural centers of the world. Her rich bicultural experience had a deep effect on her formative years.

Mexico City's ancient roots inspired her to study archaeology and pre-Columbian art at the University of the Americas in Mexico City, Mexico, after she had spent a year at the University of Arizona in Tucson, Arizona.

When she was twenty, Susan married and moved to the Pacific Northwest of the United States, where she raised two children, Lauren and Burt. Susan was a parent and part-time painter until she returned from a six-month-long trip to India, Nepal, and Thailand in 1984 and 1985—a trip that included four months studying Vedanta with Nitya Chaitanya Yati. She began collecting junk glass from second-hand stores and creating sculptures by gluing the pieces together—her first venture into three-dimensionality and mixed media.

When she discovered glass, Susan moved from Vashon Island, Washington, to Seattle and became fully ensconced in the glass world there. Later, while living in Berkeley, California, she became involved with women environmental artists and was a board member of WEAD, the Women Environmental Artists Directory started by Susan Leibowitz Steinman and Jo Hanson. Susan Plum moved back to Mexico in 2003 and stepped into social-spiritual activism with an installation for the women of Ciudad Juárez.

Susan's work is in the collections of The Corning Museum of Glass in Corning, New York; Hunter Art Museum of American Art in Chattanooga, Tennessee; ASU Art Museum in Tempe, Arizona; the World Bank; the Renwick Gallery in Washington, D.C.; Mobile Museum of Art in Mobile, Alabama; and the United States embassy in Belize.

Susan has taught at Penland School of Crafts in Penland, North Carolina; Pilchuck Glass School in Stanwood, Washington; The Studio of The Corning Museum of Glass in Corning, New York; California College of the Arts in San Francisco; Pratt Fine Arts Center in Seattle, Washington; San Jose State University in San Jose, California; and UrbanGlass in Brooklyn, New York.

Emilio Santini

The superb goblets and other glasswork of Emilio Santini are the products of his family's centuries of glassmaking history, as well as his personal journey as an artist and a man. Emilio's desire to create keeps him at the bench; even with a lifetime of learning—which dates back to his preteen years—his knowledge and technique grow with each passing year, and his work continues to achieve new levels of excellence.

Goblet, 2000
15 inches (38.1 cm)
Flameworked; glass
PHOTO BY DAVID RAMSEY

Unconscious Learning, Unwitting Privilege

I was born into a family with a 500-year-old tradition in glassblowing. I come from a tiny island of about 5,000 souls, most of whom are or have been glassblowers or involved in glass production and related fields. My father is still a glassblower, at the venerable age of eighty-eight, and still works seven days each week. My uncles, my grandfather, my brother, and one sister were all glass people. Another sister, the youngest, paid her way through college by making glass candies, and in our backyard, my mother staked her tomatoes with glass rods. Throughout my youth, I knew many entire families whose business, one way or another, was glass.

Yet, although it may seem like it was a foregone conclusion, my decision to become a glass artist came neither automatically nor early. The mere fact of coming from such glass heaven did not make me a glassblower, nor did it instill in me the will and desire to become one.

In fact, when I was growing up in Murano, Italy, the opportunity—or should I say the "unfortunate chance"—to become a glassblower was imposed on much of the younger generation as a punishment and viewed by us as almost a curse. I can still hear the words: "My son, if you do not do well in school, you'll end up working in front of the fire." Nobody wanted to spend the rest of his life slowly toasting in front of a furnace, when new opportunities—new jobs in clean, air-conditioned offices—were available if you had a degree.

Very few parents were wise enough to expose their sons to the beauty and endless possibilities of glass, because the economy was shifting from an artisan base to industry and service. My father, luckily for me, was one of the few. He loved glass and still does. He loves what he calls "that frozen, molten liquid with 365 faces, one for every day of the year," as well as glass's history, transparency, opacity, malleability, and rigidity. My great fortune is that he passed his passion on to me.

The beginning of my life in glass was not easy, though. To my father, a true education meant studying at school and also learning how hard it really is to earn a living. So, at the early age of eleven, I was offered the "choice"—in reality, the choice was imposed upon me—of spending my three months of summer vacation for the following five years in a glass factory. That first year, my teacher was my uncle, a glass master. I hated my summers, not because of the heat or the intense labor, but mostly because I knew my friends and classmates were vacationing at the beach or in the mountains while I spent my time dipping iron pipes into glowing, molten glass. It was a time of misunderstood love and misplaced hate; it was also a time of unconscious learning and unwitting privilege, as I worked shoulder to shoulder with some of the greatest *maestri* of the past century.

I constantly daydreamed of shores replete with harlequins and poetry, and I decided to follow my muse: I enrolled in Italian studies and acted semiprofessionally for 10 years. All the while,

Arteus, 2000
14 x 4½ x 4½ inches (35.5 x 11.4 x 11.4 cm)
Furnace blown, hand sculpted, lampworked; glass
PHOTO BY ARTIST
COURTESY OF HÉLÈNE AND WILLIAM SAFFIRE

Emilio Santini

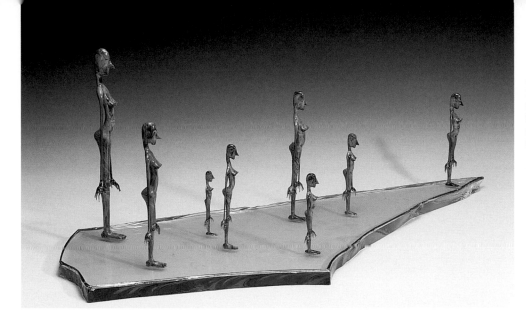

Square, 1999
10 x 25 x 12 inches
(25.4 x 63.5 x 30.5 cm)
Sculpted, lampworked;
slab glass, copper foil
PHOTO BY ARTIST

though, I was working glass in every spare moment in order to make a living. By this time, I'd switched to flameworking, which allowed me to work by myself. So, glass was still there, albeit in the background of my life, still liquid and waiting for the right opportunity to take shape. And my destiny lay elsewhere: It took a trip of thousands of miles, like the one Marco Polo took, to make me fully use my skills in a new land, while learning a new language and being supported by the love of a woman, my wife.

The United States of America is the country where glass was and is taught in colleges and universities—the place where glass was and is used as a medium to create art. In this country, I discovered the artistic freedom offered by an untouched canvas—any shape could be drawn in any color with any kind of paint. Coming from a professionally secretive environment, I was stunned by the openness of glassmakers in America. The sharing of ideas and equipment and offering of mutual respect were surprising and mind opening for me. Dreaming of success and recognition, striving for financial gain, and being blinded by ovations, I had always hated artists who copied my designs, instead of appreciating the fact that they found my work beautiful enough to imitate. But I was now on a new path of learning, along which I discovered newfound humility.

I was very lucky in that the first glass artist I met in the United States was Harvey Littleton. I visited his studio, and he helped me to understand the endless possibilities glass offered. He showed me

that tradition can sometimes be a chain that holds you prisoner to someone else's preexisting dreams. I recognized that it was time to move tradition to the back of my brain and use it as an undertone in my work, and I decided to explore new terrain in my glass objects.

Like everybody, I am a product of my desires, which can only be fulfilled and satisfied through my experiences. No one can become an artist without the desire to create. And no one can be called an artist if he is not part of that elite born with gifts for transfiguring his inner life into objects outside himself that aesthetically arrest viewers. All artists must acquire the technical skills needed to express themselves, and maybe, if they are capable, they can teach them to others. With these skills, it is possible to create beautiful, utilitarian objects, but great skills alone will not produce finished ideas. Very few people have the gift of creating true art objects, and after many years of working and making objects, I realized I am not an artist just because I call myself one.

THE PLEASURE OF MAKING

I am very fortunate to be able to make a living by working my craft—using my hands and tools to shape glass, the most ephemeral of all media, into objects. I did not fully appreciate the extent of my privilege until three years ago, when my son, then fourteen, told me how much he envied me because I could make objects and, at the end of the day, admire them, telling myself, "You made them." It is beautiful to be fully conscious of the pleasure of

THE PENLAND BOOK OF GLASS   213
Emilio Santini

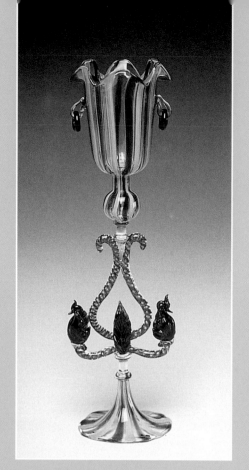

Tipetto, 2000
7 x 1½ x 1½ inches (17.8 x 3.8 x 3.8 cm)
Blown, lampworked; glass
PHOTO BY ARTIST

Incalmo Veneziano, 2005
13½ x 3½ x 3½ inches
(33 x 8.9 x 8.9 cm)
Flameworked, blown;
borosilicate glass
PHOTO BY ARTIST

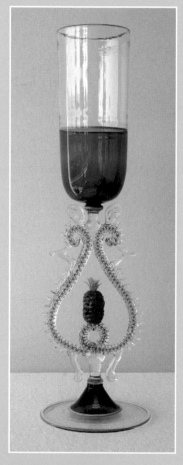

Incalmo Veneziano, 2005
12½ x 3½ x 3½ inches
(31.8 x 8.9 x 8.9 cm)
Flameworked, blown;
borosilicate glass
PHOTO BY ARTIST

Fertility Goblets, 2007
Left: 16½ x 4 x 4 inches (41.9 x 10.2 x 10.2 cm)
Right: 15 x 4 x 4 inches (38.1 x 10.2 x 10.2 cm)
Flame-sculpted, reduced; borosilicate glass
PHOTO BY ARTIST

making—of the delicious effort intrinsic to creating—and the sweet flavor of salty sweat during a hot day in front of the fire, while gently guiding glass in new directions.

Like teaching an infant to walk and talk, and then watching the child grow under your guidance, the shaping of glass into an object with its own language and its own posture gives me extreme satisfaction. It is never too hot, too cold, or too late to blow glass. I am never too tired to try new things or retry old techniques. The glass follows my prompts.

After a lifetime of exploring the material, the most satisfying thing of all for me is still the making of goblets. I often ask myself why almost all glassblowers find satisfaction in the challenge of goblet making. Maybe it is because goblets are so beautifully difficult to make, or maybe it is because these hollow containers help to fill up our sometimes empty lives.

Making goblets and tumblers is the basic foundation for most glassblowers, whether they utilize the torch or the furnace in their efforts. The dance with tools in the flame in search of the perfect goblet always produces great joy. On countless occasions, I have told my students to practice tumblers—first narrow, then wider; first smooth, then with twisted optics.

There is no path to mastery of technique other than making the objects over and over again. That is why the life of a creative person should evolve along two parallel tracks—one leading to technical skill and the other devoted to creativity and experimentation. They must exist together in a symbiotic relationship. Although one can sometimes overpower the other during the making of a specific art piece, in the end there should always be some balance, or else the piece may simply shatter into oblivion.

GLASS AS MY MATERIAL

Thorough knowledge of the material being worked is an important foundation for any craftsperson, and so it is with glassworkers. Not knowing glass's properties and "defects," or limitations, will keep an artist from using this material to its full potential.

Glass is not an element; it does not exist in nature like other materials, such as copper or iron. It can be found in only three naturally existing forms: fulgurite, the result of lightning striking sand and melting it into a glass form; obsidian, chunks of glass formed during volcanic eruptions under certain conditions; and meteorites, made up of material that comes from outer space and that melts during its entry into the Earth's atmosphere.

The basic ingredient of glass is silica, which melts at about 3182°F (1750°C). This is quite a high temperature at which to blow glass, so to lower the glass's melting point, sodium carbonate is added, and the mixture is stabilized with the addition of calcium carbonate. These are the three main ingredients in the materials used today by almost everyone who produces art-glass objects. Other minerals and oxides are added to these ingredients to refine the mixture and give it color.

There are many thousands of different kinds of glass, all beautiful, each with its own characteristics, potentials, and allure. Some have different coefficients of thermal expansion and longer or shorter working times; some have the same chemical properties but different mechanical ones; and some are even made of pure silica, which is called "quartz glass." While it would take more than a lifetime to learn everything about all the various kinds of glass, an artist should at least know all the properties of the glass he is working with in order to be able to make full use of its potential. Cracking or exploding glass-art pieces are not happy sights; knowledge can help an artist avoid such unpleasant surprises after hours of work.

In teaching, I always try to emphasize the importance of taking the time to establish a good, working knowledge base. Unfortunately, today many aspiring glassblowers quickly succumb to the seductive powers of the medium. Glass is so immediately beautiful that some people rush to acquire some technique in their hurry to create "art" straight away. But, no: It takes many years of gathering knowledge, practicing technical skills, and engaging in informed conversation with the material to become properly respectful of it. Only then, with technique and knowledge firmly established in your mind, should you let your hand follow your ideas for the manipulation of glass.

Emilio Santini

Hands On

Emilio Santini demonstrates how to make a goblet by combining flameworking and glassblowing techniques.

1   I preheat a glass tube, which I'm holding in my left hand. Holding the tube with my hand in an overhand position, rather than an underhand one, facilitates its rotation. I'm also heating the end of a punty rod.

2   After connecting the punty rod to the tubing, I pull the first point. I rotate continuously—back and forth, back and forth—to keep everything centered. If I stop rotating, gravity will pull the heated glass off-center.

3   After pulling the point, I heat up the shoulder of the tubing that is located just before the point to make it as straight as possible. When I pull the second point, I'll want everything to line up on a straight axis.

Emilio Santini

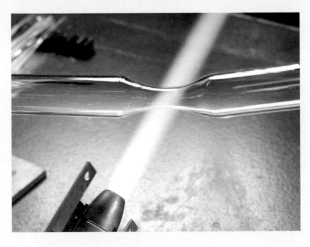

4 I reheat a second section of the tube and pull the second point. Again, my left hand is in an overhand position as it handles the glass, and my right hand is underhand. As before, I keep rotating the tube back and forth.

6 After reheating the shoulder to make sure the point is on center, I create a constriction by pressing the soft, heated glass down onto the blade that sits on top of my torch. This process, called "necking down," creates a "neck" for the bubble.

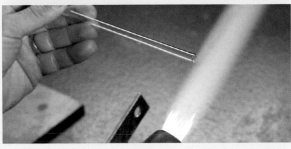

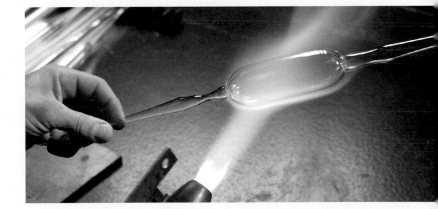

7 I heat the center tubing—the gather of glass that is between the points. The neck I created in the previous step is now positioned to the left. When the glass becomes hot enough ...

5 After I pull the second point, I score it with a piece of grinding stone and break it open. Then I fire polish the open end on one side of the flame.

8 ... I inflate the bubble by blowing through the glass point. I blow very gradually so I have time to adjust the bubble if it goes off-center. Repeatedly, I heat the piece in the flame, and when it's nice and soft, I bring it out of the flame and blow gradually until it reaches the diameter I need for my round bubble. All the while, I rotate the glass.

Emilio Santini

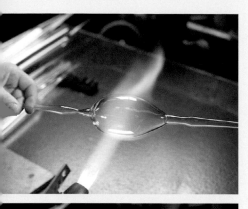

9 I put the bubble back in the flame, heat up its center, and gradually stretch it from spherical to cylindrical.

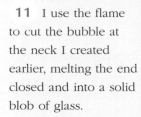

11 I use the flame to cut the bubble at the neck I created earlier, melting the end closed and into a solid blob of glass.

12 Using a graphite paddle, I flatten the still-molten end into a slightly curved disk shape. I hold the paddle at a slight angle to the glass.

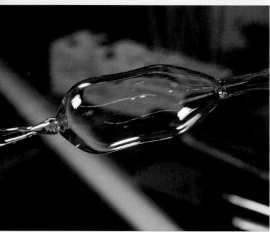

10 Note that there's a convex area in the middle of the bubble. I reheat the bubble in the flame and give a little puff to straighten out the walls. I keep repeating these processes—putting the bubble in the flame, blowing gradually, pulling, and rotating all the while—until I get the piece where I want it to be.

13 I apply another gather, or molten bead, of glass to the disk with a clear rod. I flatten the end with a graphite paddle.

14 I heat the neck of the glass and use jacks to create an *avoglio*, a bobbin-like shape. I then attach a punty to this end.

15 I reorient the piece, switching the *avoglio* end to my left hand. I heat up the other point; this end will become the top of the goblet's cup.

16 To create a round shape on the top of the bubble, I heat it up and blow through the glass point so that the end of the bubble connected to the open glass point becomes roundly curved like a dome. I'm rotating the glass continuously.

17 I heat the point and use diamond shears to squeeze the glass down to a smaller diameter—about ¼ inch (6 mm) in this case. After the glass solidifies, I forcefully squeeze the glass with diamond shears to score it.

18 Still holding the glass with my diamond shears, I tap the far end of the point on top of my jacks so that the glass breaks off at the score line.

19 I heat the opening in the flame.

Emilio Santini

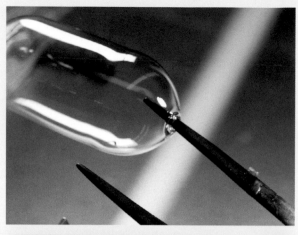

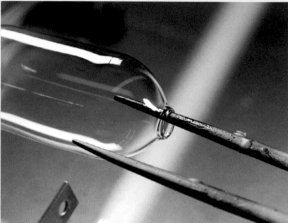

20 I insert one end of my jacks and start widening the opening to create a lip.

21 Working with a reduced flame, I apply a colored stringer to the lip.

22 After I apply the stringer, a bit of extra material always remains on the glass. Here, I cut it off. I then reheat the lip and smooth it on a graphite paddle.

23 I boost the flame and hold the glass in it almost vertically, while rotating the glass continuously.

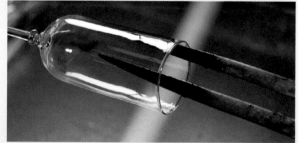

24 When the glass becomes soft, I move it to a more horizontal plane. I insert both blades of the jacks and start enlarging the opening of the cup while rotating the glass back and forth.

25 I sometimes flatten down the edge of the cup with a graphite paddle. Usually, if everything has been centered properly, this step is unnecessary.

26 The top of the goblet has been completed.

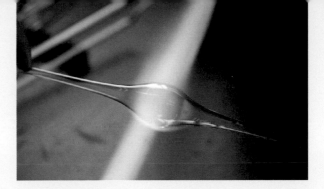

27 I prepare a much shorter gather of glass between two points; I'll be using this glass to make the foot of the goblet. I repeat the processes used for the cup: pulling points, cutting one open, fire polishing, and reheating in the flame, rotating all the while.

28 I start to inflate the glass. My goal is to make this bubble squat, rather than round.

29 I neck down the piece to create an indentation with the blade mounted atop my torch, and I cut the glass off using the flame. I then flatten the neck on a graphite paddle, add a gather of glass to the end with a clear glass rod, flatten it again with the graphite paddle, create an *avoglio* with jacks, and add a punty to this end—identical processes to the ones I performed on the top of the cup. I also score the end opposite the *avoglio* with diamond shears and break it open at the score line.

30 I work the opening with one end of the jacks and apply a stringer to the rim. I then trim any excess with shears.

31 I heat the opening, put in both ends of my jacks, and start to flare open the foot. I switch from metal jacks to graphite jacks during this process.

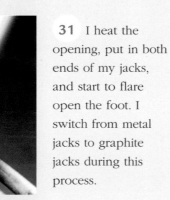

32 The foot of the goblet has been completed.

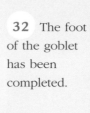

33 Next, I create the stem. I pull two points on heavy-walled tubing with a smaller diameter, centering everything so it's as straight as possible. I heat up a section of tubing about ½ inch (1.3 cm) from one of the points. When it's very hot, I neck down lightly—while rotating the glass—to create an indentation; I create two separate sections that are still open to each other in the middle of the piece. I heat the smaller section and gently blow to form the shape I desire; I also neck down on its outer edge for the same purpose.

34 I reorient the piece by switching hands. I heat up the longer section of the stem so that it becomes very soft, and I stretch it, while rotating it continuously. I neck down to create another indentation.

35 The stem has been completed.

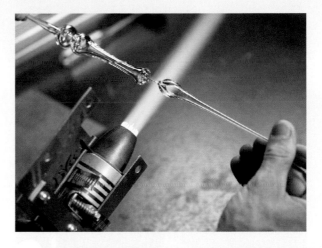

36 I disconnect the bottom point from the stem.

37 I place the goblet's foot in a grabber. I heat the end of the foot's *avoglio* and the end of the stem, and I fuse the stem to the goblet's base.

Emilio Santini

38 Holding the foot, now with the stem attached, in the grabber, I use the diamond shears to score and disconnect the remaining point. I take care not to squeeze too much because I want an open hole to remain in the stem; otherwise, if gasses expanded without anywhere to go, they would rip open a hole on the side of the stem.

39 I soften the very bottom of the *avoglio* on the bottom of the cup, as well as the very top of the stem, to an almost liquid point.

40 I bring the cup down vertically on top of the stem and squeeze down slowly to join the two pieces. I rotate the glass as the pieces join to ensure that the entire piece is centered and straight; I make adjustments as necessary. All this happens in about three seconds—which is relatively slow for glasswork! Attaching the pieces vertically makes it much easier to keep everything centered, so gravity does not distort the connection.

Emilio Santini

About the Artist

Emilio Santini was born in Murano, Italy, in 1955, as part of a noble family with a centuries-old glassblowing tradition. His father, Mario Santini, was his first teacher in Venetian glassblowing. At the age of eleven, Emilio was sent to work in a glass factory during the three-month summer break from school; his uncle, Giacinto Cadamuro, was his teacher. During each of the next five years, he went back to work for three months in the same glass factory, but with different masters. When Emilio was seventeen, his father started teaching him flameworking, and he became a full-time torchworker at age twenty-three.

Emilio says his extensive teaching at major American glass schools has helped him expand his view of the world of art glass, and studying with William Gudenrath, resident advisor at The Corning Museum of Glass in Corning, New York, allowed him to progress even further with his skill at the bench. While Emilio's work is quite broad in its scope, encompassing furnace and torch work, casting, blowing, sculpting, and engraving, and ranging from delicate miniatures to 8-foot (2.4 m) chandeliers, flameworked goblets are the ever-present and ever-evolving core of his artistic repertoire.

Emilio is part of the glass faculty at Virginia Commonwealth University in Richmond, Virginia, and he has taught at Penland School of Crafts in Penland, North Carolina; Pilchuck School of Glass in Stanwood, Washington; Pittsburgh Glass Center in Pittsburgh, Pennsylvania; The Studio of The Corning Museum of Glass in Corning, New York; UrbanGlass in Brooklyn, New York; and Pratt Fine Arts Center in Seattle, Washington.

He is represented internationally by some of the world's leading galleries, and he is featured in numerous private and museum collections, including The Corning Museum of Glass; the Museum of Contemporary Art in Venice, Italy; the Mint Museum of Craft and Design in Charlotte, North Carolina; the Chrysler Museum of Art in Norfolk, Virginia; and the Kentucky Museum of Art and Craft in Louisville, Kentucky.

In 1988, Emilio moved with his wife to Williamsburg, Virginia, where they reside with their son and daughter.

Tipetto, 2000
8 x 2 x 2 inches (20.3 x 5.1 x 5.1 cm)
Blown, lampworked; glass
PHOTO BY ARTIST
COURTESY OF THE MINT MUSEUM, CHARLOTTE, NORTH CAROLINA

Uros, 2000
14 x 4½ x 4½ inches
(35.6 x 11.4 x 11.4 cm)
Blown, sandblasted,
hand-painted, lampworked,
sculpted; glass
PHOTO BY ARTIST

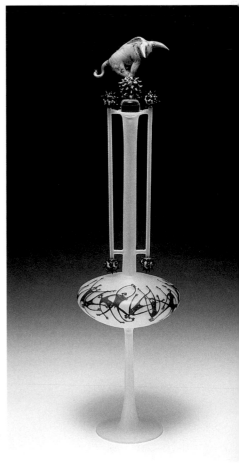

Penland School of Crafts Overview

Penland School of Crafts is a national center for craft education located in the mountains of North Carolina. Penland's mission is to support individual and artistic growth through craft. Penland offers one-, two-, and eight-week adult workshops in books and paper, clay, drawing and painting, glass, iron, metals, photography, printmaking, textiles, and wood. The school also sponsors artists' residencies and a community education program and runs a craft gallery representing artists affiliated with the school.

Penland School was founded by Lucy Morgan, a teacher at an Episcopalian school that once occupied several buildings still in use by Penland today. In 1923, Morgan organized the Penland Weavers, which provided looms, materials, and instruction to local women and marketed their handwoven goods. She invited weaving expert Edward F. Worst to teach, and when requests for instruction came from other parts of the country,

Penland School was born. Soon after the first students arrived in 1929, other crafts were added, and the school began to raise funds, acquire property, and construct buildings.

When Morgan retired in 1962, she was succeeded by Bill Brown. During Brown's 21-year tenure, new media, such as iron and glass, were added to the program, and the school began offering eight-week sessions in the spring and fall. Brown also started the resident-artist program, which provides low-cost housing and studios to craft artists who work at Penland for several years, and he began a work-study scholarship program to make Penland accessible to a broader range of students.

Today, the school encompasses 49 buildings located on 400 acres of land. Each year approximately 1,200 people come to Penland for instruction, and another 14,000 pass through as visitors. Penland has no standing faculty; its instructors include full-time studio artists and teachers from

colleges and universities. Students live at Penland and take only one class at a time, allowing them to learn by total immersion; the ideas and information gained in a two-week session might take a year to absorb and process.

The school has also become the focal point for a lively community of craft artists, thanks in part to the resident-artist program, which has encouraged many artists to settle in the area. The presence of so many nearby studios greatly enhances the quality of the student experience.

Students come from all walks of life. They range from nineteen to ninety years of age and from absolute beginners to professional craftspeople. Students sometimes view Penland as a productive retreat, as a source of inspiration for their personal creative lives, or as a place to exchange vital information about process and techniques. What brings all these students together is a love of materials and making, and the often transformative experience of working with intensity and focus in a supportive community atmosphere.

Penland School began out of a strong belief in a few simple values. Lucy Morgan summarized them as "the joy of creative occupation and a certain togetherness—working with one another in creating the good and the beautiful." For more than 75 years, these principles have guided a remarkable institution that has had a pervasive influence on American craft and touched the lives of thousands of individuals.

For more information about Penland School of Crafts, visit www.penland.org.

Acknowledgments

This book is an extraordinary labor of love produced by a diverse array of committed professionals, including glass artists, photographers, and staff at Penland School of Crafts and Lark Books. This team worked together diligently for a year and a half to create the volume you hold in your hands, which is the fifth release in Lark Books' collaborative series with Penland School of Crafts. Earlier volumes were dedicated to ceramics, handmade books, jewelry, and woodworking.

The magic of the book starts with the featured artists and teachers: Vittorio Costantini, Shane Fero, Ingalena Klenell, Kristina Logan, Elizabeth Ryland Mears, Janis Miltenberger, Susan Plum, Sally Prasch, Emilio Santini, and Paul Stankard. Their mastery is evidenced not just in their outstanding flamework, which is so well represented in the book, but also in their passion for teaching and sharing their technical and philosophical approaches to glass, art, and life. I spoke almost daily with many of these artists over the past year and a half, and their dedication to this project never failed to amaze me; the artists treated their chapters as works of art in themselves. Their effort is reflected in the thoughtfulness and beauty of their writing.

The first-rate work of all the photographers is a key to the book's quality and comprehensiveness. We appreciate the artists and institutions that contributed gallery images, which expand and elaborate on the possibilities flameworking holds, and offer a special thanks to Shane Fero for his great assistance curating the book's gallery selections.

Jean W. McLaughlin, director of Penland School of Crafts, enthusiastically endorsed the book, and other key Penland staff members were instrumental in bringing it to publication. Our thanks go to Dana Moore, Penland program director, and Robin Dreyer, Penland communications manager; they acted as the school's primary liaisons through the book's many months of production. Slate Grove, Penland glass studio coordinator, and Simone Travisano, studio manager, reviewed the book, and Sally Prasch served as technical reader.

At Lark Books, Beth Sweet was developmental assistant for the book; her kind, empathetic approach kept materials flowing in from artists and photographers, and her organizational innovation made that flow much more manageable. Linda Kopp and Amanda Carestio formed an outstanding production editorial team, and Chris Rich, Dawn Dillingham, Rosemary Kast, Shannon Quinn-Tucker, and Meghan Wanucha all contributed essential, excellent editorial work. Art director Kristi Pfeffer designed two earlier books in the series, and I'm convinced her wonderful design reaches a new height in this volume. Kristi was ably assisted in layout by Avery Johnson, and Shannon Yokeley led and coordinated the rest of the fine art production team, which included Jeff Hamilton, Craig Shapley, and Nicole Minkin.

Ray Hemachandra, *Senior Editor*

Contributing Photographers

Esmé Alexander of Hagersten, Sweden, photographed Ingalena Klenell in her studio in Edsbjörke, Sunne, in Sweden.

Paul Avis of Portsmouth, New Hampshire, photographed Kristina Logan in her studio in Portsmouth.

Carol Bates of Philadelphia, Pennsylvania, photographed Paul Stankard in his studio in Mantua, New Jersey.

Robert de Gast of San Miguel de Allende, Mexico, photographed Susan Plum in her studio in San Miguel de Allende. Susan's portrait photograph was taken by **Linda Robbins**.

Robin Dreyer of Burnsville, North Carolina, photographed the images that accompany the introduction, the overview of Penland School of Crafts, and the acknowledgments.

Pete Duvall of Silver Spring, Maryland, photographed Elizabeth Ryland Mears in her studio in Fairfax Station, Virginia.

Steve Horn of Lopez Island, Washington, photographed Janis Miltenberger in her studio on Lopez Island. **Lynn Thompson** of Seattle, Washington, photographed the beauty shot of Janis' finished piece and her portrait photograph.

Gian Mauro Lapenna photographed Vittorio Costantini in his studio in Venice, Italy.

Steve Mann photographed Sally Prasch and Emilio Santini in the glass studio at Penland School of Crafts and Shane Fero in his home studio in Penland, North Carolina.

Contributing Artists

Daniel Adams
Seattle, Washington
Pages 72–73

Alex Arbell
Ein-Hod, Israel
Page 76

Rick Ayotte
New Boston, New Hampshire
Page 175

Bennett Battaile
Portland, Oregon
Pages 160–161

Tina Betz
Clayville, New York
Page 172

Frederick Birkhill
Pickney, Michigan
Page 166

Lucio Bubacco
Murano, Venice
Page 167

Victor Chiarizia
Fairview, North Carolina
Page 71

Richard Clements
Franklin, Tasmania
Page 77

Bandhu Scott Dunham
Prescott, Arizona
Page 165

Kathleen Elliot
Santa Clara, California
Pages 78–79

Matthew Eskuche
Pittsburgh, Pennsylvania
Page 68

Hans Godo Frabel
Atlanta, Georgia
Page 158

Albrecht Greiner-Mai
Lauscha, Germany
Page 58

Andre Gutgesell
Ernstthal, Germany
Pages 60–61

Doni Hatz
Loveland, Ohio
Page 174

Tom Holland
Fox, Arizona
Page 63

Shari Maxson Hopper
Paradise, California
Page 67

Dinah Hulet
McKinleyville, California
Page 66

Marshall Hyde
Corning, New York
Page 155

Amy Johnson
Toronto, Ontario, Canada
Page 171

Helena Kågebrand
Stockholm, Sweden
Pages 158–159

Brian Kerkvliet
Bellingham, Washington
Page 175

Hubert Koch
Ernstthal, Germany
Page 172

Masami Koda
Bothell, Washington
Pages 64–65

Donald Lipski
Philadelphia, Pennsylvania
Page 177

Carmen Lozar
Normal, Illinois
Pages 74–75

Christopher McElroy
Missoula, Montana
Page 159

Kate Fowle Meleney
Sauderstown, Rhode Island
Pages 80–81

Robert Mickelsen
Melbourne, Florida
Pages 170–171

James Minson
Seattle, Washington
Pages 156–157

Jillian Molettiere
Swedesboro, New Jersey
Page 154

Milissa Montini
Aliquippa, Pennsylvania
Pages 82–83

Thomas Muller-Litz
Lauscha, Germany
Page 61

Jay Musler
Oakland, California
Pages 59–60

Pat Owens
North Wales, Pennsylvania
Pages 178–179

Mark Peiser
Penland, North Carolina
Pages 70–71

Judith Pfaff
Kingston, New York
Page 164

Nathan R. Purcell
Philadelphia, Pennsylvania
Page 69

Jill Reynolds
Beacon, New York
Pages 162–163

JDC Roman
Eddyville, Oregon
Page 176

Ginny Ruffner
Seattle, Washington
Pages 84–85

Kari Russell-Pool
Centerbrook, Connecticut
Page 153

Priscilla Turner Spada
Newburyport, Massachusetts
Page 62

Wayne Strattman
Boston, Massachusetts
Pages 168–169

Loren Stump
Elk Grove, California
Pages 152–153

Gianni Toso
Baltimore, Maryland
Page 173

Heather Trimlett
El Cajon, California
Page 62

Kathryn Wardill
Melbourne, Victoria
Page 72

Harumi Yukutake
Hachioji, Tokyo
Page 176

Index